MW01097929

# Denver and Rio Grande Western
## Superpower Railroad of the Rockies

### by Robert A. LeMassena

ROYAL GORGE
MOFFAT TUNNEL
SCENIC LINE OF THE WORLD

1999
TLC Publishing Inc. ~ 1387 Winding Creek Lane ~ Lynchburg, VA 24503-3776

TLC
PUBLISHING INC.

## Front Cover Illustration:

The sixteen miles of the Colorado River's Ruby Canyon between Mack, Colorado, and Westwater, UT, is extremely beautiful but also very remote. Until quite recent times the only known photos were taken around 1901. Although all of the D&RGW's super-power locomotives were operated through the canyon every day for thirty years, it seems there are no photos of any of them there. Among the Rio Grande's locomotives the 3-cylinder 4-8-2s (1600s) were the least photographed; they had been scrapped before railfans had discovered them. Hence the 1602, hauling a freight train through the canyon, would be a rare scene, one which no one, other than D&RGW employees, had ever witnessed. Gil Bennett's painting, based on an Otto Perry photo from 1939 and Jim Ozments's recent photos of the canyon, brings to our eyes a most unusual panorama of the Rio Grande in an almost unknown location.

## Front Endsheet

After stopping for water at Funston, across the Colorado River from Glenwood Springs, 2-8+8-2, No. 3614 at the head of an eastbound freigh train begins the 18-mile climb up the 1.6% grade through steep-walled Glenwood Canyon to Dotsero. Although the Scenic Limited is only a few minutes behind it, the powerful articulated will be running over the cutoff line toward the Moffat Tunnel before the long passenger tain could reach the junction and head for Tennessee Pass.

LeMassena

## Rear Endsheet

No. 3606 was hauling a solid trainload of finished lumber, which had originated on the Western Pacific in California in the circa 1930 view at Castle Rock..
George Beam/D&RGW Collection
Couresy of Jackson Thode

# Table of Contents

© Copyright 1999
TLC Publishing, Inc.

All rights reserved.
No part of this book may be reproduced without written permission from the publisher, except for brief excerpts used in reviews, etc.

Library of Congress Catalogue
Card Number 99-73810
ISBN 1-883089-48-4

Layout and Design
by Kenneth L. Miller
Miller Design & Photography, Salem, Va.

Printed by
Walsworth Publishing Co.
Marceline, Mo. 64658

# *Acknowledgements*

Charles Albi, Director of the Colorado Railroad Museum, provided the ICC and D&RGW reports on the 3703's catastrophe.

Robert Andrews, a local railfan, supplied photos of trains in uncommon locations.

Kenton Forrest, Librarian of the Colorado Railroad Museum, helped locate unusual photos of Rio Grande trains.

Rocky Haimowitz, a local expert on locomotive boilers, analyzed the accident reports concerning engine No. 3703.

Kevin Keefe, Editor of TRAINS Magazine, generously permitted use of the original manuscript about the 3703's last trip.

Thomas Klinger, a local photographer, produced excellent prints from Bob Andrew's, Dick Kindig's and Neal Miller's negatives.

Richard Kindig, a famous railfan photographer, supplied some of his incomparable action photos.

Dell McCoy, President of Sundance Publications, advised about new photo reproduction techniques.

Kenneth Miller, book designer, who assembled the text, photos, tables, and diagrams to form an attractive volume.

Neal Miller, another local railfan, supplied excellent examples of his camera work.

James Ozment, retired D&RGW Division Engineer, provided wonderful insight regarding D&RGW motive power and track structure policies.

Jackson Thode, retired Chief Budget Officer of the railroad, whose vast collection and knowledge of everything "Rio Grande", were consulted on numerous occasions.

Harold Vollrath, a retired Missouri Pacific dispatcher, furnished a great majority of the photos, made from negatives in his enormous collection.

My wife, Betty, whose adventures include riding on the 3619 up Tennessee Pass, touring the Monarch branch on narrow-gauge No. 484, and coasting down Son-of-a-Gun Hill on Manitou & Pike's Peak No. 6; for her patiently listening to my revelations concerning Gresley conjugated-lever valve-gear, effective drawbar-pull and combustion-chamber syphons.

# *Photographs*

Within the past decade, several collections of negatives and prints have "disappeared" for all practical purposes. Some collections have been dissipated into the hands of other railfans or public institutions. Other collections have passed to heirs, whose locations are unknown. Preservation organizations have indexed files of photos, but one must visit them in person to find out what is needed. There are, however, individuals such as Harold Vollrath who can locate the negative for a particular locomotive and supply a print for examination or publication. Now, some institutions are supplying computer-scanned prints of low definition or prints from copy-negatives which have lost detail in shadow and highlight areas. These two kinds of prints are unsuitable for high quality production and are no better than re-scanned halftone screened reproductions. If an original print cannot be obtained, using a printed reproduction might be the only way to obtain a suitable illustration; in some instances that technique has been used in this publication. This is an unfortunate situation, yet it is better than nothing at all.

## Photographic Sources

ALC - American Locomotive Company/Alco Historic Photos
CRMS - Colorado Railroad Museum Collection
CVC - C. V. Colstadt/CRMC
HKV - Harold K. Vollrath
HKVC - Harold K. Vollrath Collection
HRG - Henry R. Griffiths/CRMC
LEM - LeMassena
LEMC - LeMassena Collection
NRM - Neal R. Miller
OCP - Otto C. Perry/Denver Public Library
RTS - Richard T. Steinheimer
REC - Robert Edwards Collection
RBG - Ross B. Grenard
RHK - Richard H. Kindig
RHKC - Richard H. Kindig Collection
RRA - Railroad Archives/Jackson C. Thode
RWA - Robert W. Andrews
RWR - Robert W. Richardson

# *Introduction* 1881-1889

nlike most other railroads, the Rio Grande changed every aspect of its corporate character during the first century of its existence. Its ultimate destination, track gauge, profile, motive power, rolling stock, traffic and even its name experienced monumental modifications at one time or another. Originally planned as a 3-foot gauge railway running some 1600 miles from Denver, CO. to Mexico City, the railroad evolved into an east-west bridge route between Denver/Pueblo and Ogden/Salt Lake City. Its earliest locomotives were tiny 2-4-0s and 2-6-0s; fifty years later its locomotives were among the heaviest and largest of their types, and they were rarely surpassed.

The causes of the continual motive power metamorphosis were the manifold changes in the Rio Grande's route and traffic. Each phase of the railroad's development resembled an episode in a Saturday afternoon serial-movie thriller, and the outcome was no more predictable. The Denver and Rio Grande Railway commenced construction southward from Denver in 1871, and by 1877 its track had extended 213 miles to a coal mine near Trinidad, CO. There, further construction was blocked by the Santa Fe, which had occupied Raton Pass, the only practical route into New Mexico. Abandoning its Mexican intentions, the D&RG expanded rapidly westward from Pueblo and La Veta, CO, into the mountainous southwest quadrant of Colorado, where a great metal mining and smelting boom was

taking place. The railroad became the principal artery of transportation in that vast area. By 1881 the rails had reached almost every productive location, and in the next year a mainline had been extended across the Continental Divide to Grand Junction at Milepost 424 miles from Denver.

At this point in time the D&RG's initial development was essentially complete, though the locations of the various principal lines and branches deviated considerably from those shown on the map filed with the corporation documents. The motive power roster embraced six wheel- arrangements: 0-6-0T, 2-4-0, 2-6-0, 2-8-0, 4-4-0, and 4-6-0, all built by Baldwin, plus a single 0-4-4-0T Fairlie from England.

As this first era ended a new and much different one had already begun. In 1881 a third rail was added to the track between Denver and Pueblo to accommodate passenger trains of the Santa Fe, as well as the products of the iron and steel mill near Pueblo. Thus began the conversion of the D&RG's mainline track to standard gauge, an undertaking which would take a decade to complete. Between Salida and Glenwood Springs, the long branch became part of the new mainline into Grand Junction, and the original mainline through Gunnison

After stopping for water at Funston, across the Colorado River from Glenwood Springs, 2-8+8-2, No. 3614 at the head of an eastbound freigh train begins the 18-mile climb up the 1.6% grade through steep-walled Glenwood Canyon to Dotsero. Although the Scenic Limited is only a few minutes behind it, the powerful articulated will be running over the cutoff line toward the Moffat Tunnel before the long passenger tain could reach the junction and head for Tennessee Pass. LeMassena

# Condensed Profile of the Main Line via Pueblo

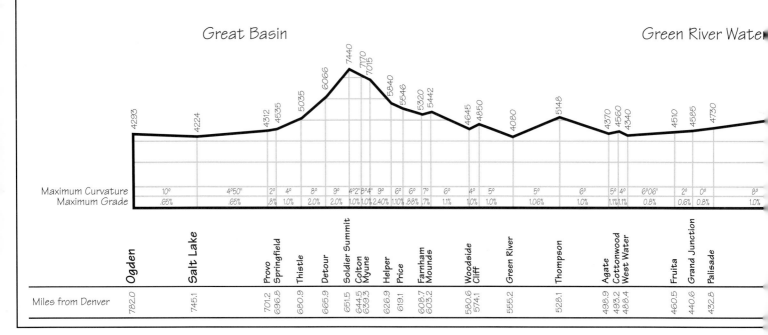

became part of a narrow-gauge system, an entity unto itself. Although 26 miles longer, the standard-gauge route was much faster.

While all this was taking place in Colorado, a new company, the Denver & Rio Grande Western Railway, had been acquiring small railroads in the vicinity of Salt Lake City. A mainline, connecting these little railroads was thrust eastward across the desert, and at the same time, track was being laid westward from Grand Junction. When the two lines met west of Green River, UT, in 1883, a narrow-gauge route, 735 miles long, connected Denver and Salt Lake City. Despite the D&RG's gradual conversion of its mainline to standard gauge, the D&RGW behaved otherwise, and it continued to operate as a westward extension of the D&RG's narrow-gauge system through 1889, when a new company, the Rio Grande Western, was formed to take over the D&RGW and execute the conversion to standard gauge track.

The D&RGW's motive power was both ridiculous and pathetic, and it never owned a new engine. Seven 0-6-0s, a 2-6-0 and a 4-4-0 had been inherited from the acquired railroads in Utah, plus 22 2-8-0s, three 4-6-0s, and two 4-4-0s which had come from the D&RG. All of these narrow-gauge engines would become surplus when the D&RGW's track was changed to standard gauge.

During the 1890s the RGW and D&RG converted more trackage to standard gauge, a process which lasted several years. The D&RG had 3-rail track into Denver until 1901, and between Salida and Leadville until 1921. On these segments standard-gauge locomotives pulled narrow-gauge cars. There was no economic reason to convert the lines south and west of Salida; so, this narrow-gauge system was operated as though it were a separate railroad, and it remained virtually intact for a great many years.

The D&RG continued to purchase its engines—2-6-0s, 4-6-0s and 2-8-0s—from Baldwin, while the RGW obtained similar locomotives from other manufacturers. This motive

*vi*

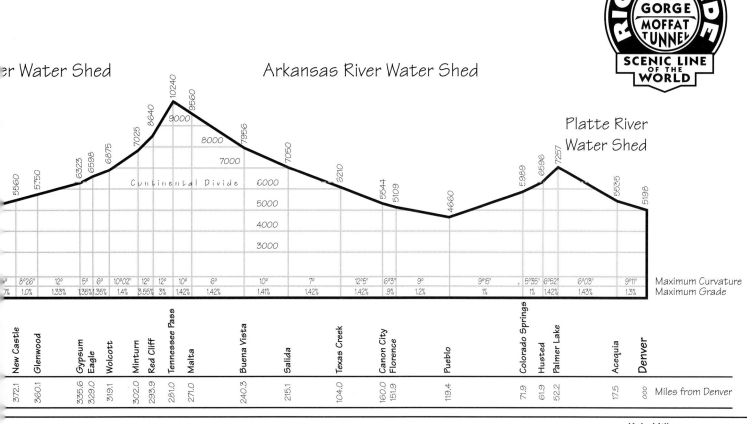

Water Shed          Arkansas River Water Shed

Platte River Water Shed

Continental Divide

Elevations (feet): 5560, 5750, 6323, 6598, 6875, 7025, 8640, 9000, 10240, 9560, 8000, 7956, 7050, 7000, 6000, 5210, 5544, 5109, 5000, 4660, 4000, 3000, 5989, 6596, 7257, 5535, 5198

| Station | Maximum Curvature | Maximum Grade | Miles from Denver |
|---|---|---|---|
| New Castle | 8°26" | 1.0% | 372.1 |
| Glenwood | 12° | 1.33% | 360.1 |
| Gypsum | 5° | 1.35% | 335.6 |
| Eagle | 6° | 1.35% | 329.0 |
| Wolcott | 10°02" | 1.4% | 319.1 |
| Minturn | 12° | 3.55% | 302.0 |
| Red Cliff | 12° | 3% | 293.9 |
| Tennessee Pass | 10° | 1.42% | 281.0 |
| Malta | 6° | 1.42% | 271.0 |
| Buena Vista | 10° | 1.41% | 240.3 |
| Salida | 7° | 1.42% | 215.1 |
| Texas Creek | 12°5" | 1.42% | 104.0 |
| Canon City | 6°3" | .9% | 160.0 |
| Florence | 9° | 1.2% | 151.9 |
| Pueblo | 9°15" | 1% | 119.4 |
| Colorado Springs | 5°35" | 1% | 71.9 |
| Husted | 6°52" | 1.42% | 61.9 |
| Palmer Lake | 6°03" | 1.43% | 52.2 |
| Acequia | 9°11" | 1.3% | 17.5 |
| Denver | | | 000 |

K. L. Miller

power diversity ended in 1899, when George Gould (son of Jay Gould, the railroad financier) obtained financial and managerial control of the two railroads. Thereafter, "standard" 0-6-0s, 4-6-0s and 2-8-0s, would be purchased, mostly from American. This concept lasted about a decade, the last 4-6-0s having arrived in 1909 and the last 2-8-0s in 1908, when the RGW and D&RG were formally merged as the Denver & Rio Grande Railroad. Almost immediately it became evident that the profiles and traffic of the "Utah Lines" and "Colorado Lines" were so different that different motive power would be required to handle the freight and passenger trains. Both the Colorado and Utah lines originated large tonnages of coal and metalliferous ores and concentrates, but the logistics of their movement were so different that much more powerful engines than 2-8-0s were required. After 1910, when the Western Pacific was completed between Salt Lake City and Oakland, CA, merchandise traffic began to flow over the D&RG between the Missouri Pacific at Pueblo to the western Pacific. Added to all of this traffic was a substantial volume of agricultural products originating in both states. Hence, the development of the Rio Grande's remarkable locomotive really begins at this date.

During the traffic surge in the fall of 1949, 4-8-2 No. 1503 brought a freight train from Grand Junction to Glenwood Springs, where 2-8+8-2 No. 3613 was added for the ascent to Minturn. There, two more 3600s were cut into the formation to climb the 3% grade to Tennessee Pass. In this panorama at Mitchell, a couple of miles north of the summit tunnel, the entire ensemble was seen entering the big S-curve at a spectacular 10 m.p.h. (LeMassena)

# *Big Engines For A New Era* 1910-1921

## 1

When the D&RG constructed the Western Pacific as the western extension of the Missouri Pacific-Rio Grande system, it utilized its own revenues and other financial resources. In addition, it agreed to guarantee payment of the WP's debt as well as its operating expenses until the WP could be self-supporting. Not only did this deprive the D&RG of funds which it needed for track improvements and new motive power, but also the D&RG was setting the stage for its own demise. Expenditures for locomotives and operating improvements were postponed until situations became intolerable. Three areas were particularly troublesome: the 3% grade on the northern side of Tennessee Pass, the 4% grade on the western flank of Soldier Summit, and the enormous tonnage of copper ore and concentrates coming out of the mines at Bingham, UT. Mainline passenger trains were frequently double-headed with 4-6-0s, which needed a pair of 2-8-0s to ascend the grades. Three 2-8-0s were needed to boost short freight trains uphill. Moreover, Utah coal had to be hoisted up a 2.4% gradient on the eastern approach to Soldier Summit.

Relief finally arrived in 1910 when the WP was completed, in the form of eight 2-6+6-2 Mallet articulateds from American. Weighing 340,000 lbs., they could exert a 62000-lb. tractive effort. Their driving wheels were the same diameter as those of the newest 2-8-0s, but only 10% larger grate area, which was inadequate for such an engine. Other features, typical of the time, were the inside-bearing trailing truck, slide valves for the low-pressure cylinders, and piston-valves for the high-pressure cylinders, which were supplied with saturated steam. Many years later their boilers were rebuilt with superheaters. Bearing numbers 1050-1057 originally, they were assigned to Tennessee Pass and Soldier Summit helper service, where they were found to have been too small. Three years later they were superseded by 2-8+8-2s, and were assigned to branch lines in Utah, where they remained until their retirement in 1946-1952.

The completion of the Western Pacific in 1910 introduced a new pattern of traffic flow-merchandise and machinery from the

*The 1195, demoted to yard switching, as were many other 2-8-0s, was assembling a narrow-gauge train at Salida, CO., in 1955, just a year before the railroad concluded all standard-gauge steam-power operations. RWR*

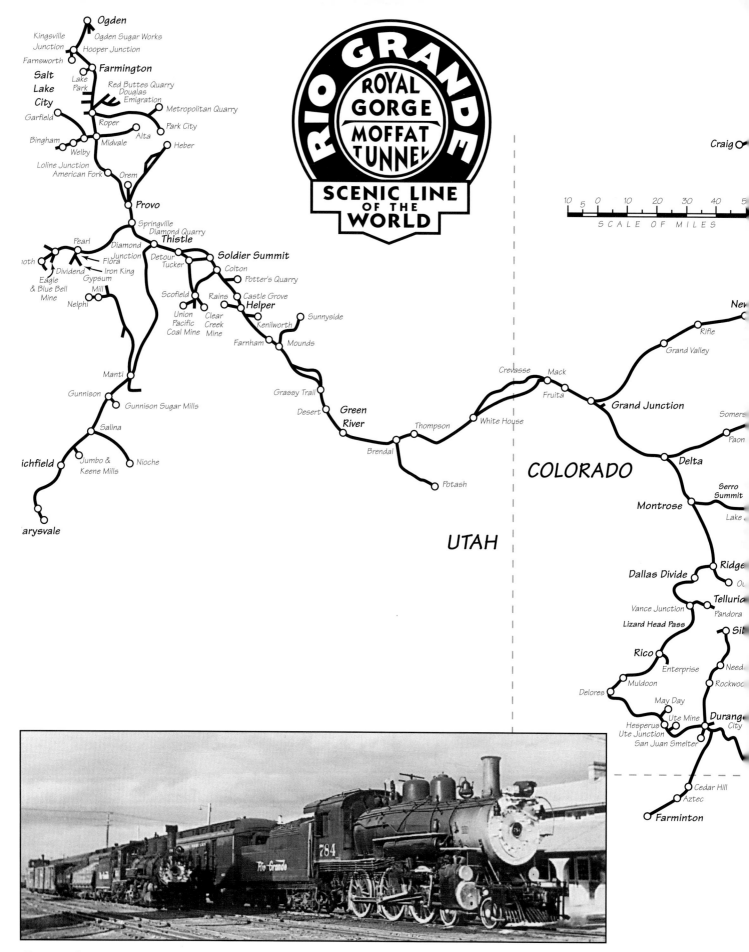

**RIO GRANDE**
ROYAL GORGE MOFFAT TUNNEL
SCENIC LINE OF THE WORLD

Ogden
Kingsville Junction
Ogden Sugar Works
Hooper Junction
Farnsworth
**Farmington**
Salt Lake City
Lake Park
Red Buttes Quarry
Douglas
Emigration
Metropolitan Quarry
Garfield
Roper
Park City
Bingham
Alta
Welby
Midvale
Heber
Loline Junction
American Fork
Orem
Provo
Springville
Diamond Quarry
Pearl
**Thistle**
Diamond Junction
Detour
**Soldier Summit**
10th
Flora
Tucker
Colton
Dividend
Iron King
Potter's Quarry
Eagle & Blue Bell Mine
Gypsum
Mill
Scofield
Rains
Castle Grove
Nelphi
Union Pacific Coal Mine
Clear Creek Mine
**Helper**
Kenilworth
Sunnyside
Manti
Farnham
Mounds
Gunnison
Gunnison Sugar Mills
Grassy Trail
Salina
Desert
**Green River**
ichfield
Jumbo & Keene Mills
Nioche
Thompson
White House
Brendal
Crevasse
Mack
Fruita
arysvale
Potash
**Grand Junction**

Craig O
New
Rifle
Grand Valley
Somers
**COLORADO**
Paon
**Delta**
Serro Summit
**Montrose**
Lake
**UTAH**
Ridge
**Dallas Divide**
Ou
**Telluria**
Vance Junction
Pandora
Lizard Head Pass
Si
**Rico**
Enterprise
Need
Muldoon
Rockwoo
Delores
May Day
Ute Mine
**Durang**
Hesperus
Ute Junction
City
San Juan Smelter
Cedar Hill
Aztec
O **Farminton**

10 5 0 10 20 30 40 5
SCALE OF MILES

For more than a quarter century (1881-1913) the Rio Grande hauled its standard-gauge rains with 4-6-0s and 2-8-0s, the last of which were delivered in 1909 and 1908, respectively. The 784 is shown at Montrose, CO. in 1952, just prior to its retirement. At the left is a narrow-gauge 2-8-2 No. 464, ready to depart for Ridgeway. CRMC

Missouri Pacific at Pueblo, and lumber and perishables from the Western Pacific at Salt Lake City. The D&RG was thus a bridge line between the other two railroads, and transit time became an important operating aspect. The 1906-1908 model 2-8-0s, with 57-inch drivers were incapable of moving the traffic rapidly enough; so, the D&RG bought fourteen new 2-8-2s from Baldwin in 1912 for this service. Despite their 63-inch drivers, their tractive effort was 25% greater, and their 63 sq. ft. grate area gave them a 50% greater steam production. These engines, numbered 1200-1213, were equipped with superheaters and fabricated-frame trailing trucks. Initially they were handicapped by lack of a mechanical stoker, an appliance which was added in the late 1930s. They were the principal mainline freight power until 1922, when they were replaced with much larger 4-8-2s.

During the next fifteen years they hauled mainline freight trains between Denver and Salida, Glenwood Springs and Green River, and Ogden and Provo. In 1934 a 42-mile cutoff line was constructed, linking the Denver and Salt Lake railroad at Orestod with the Rio Grande at Dotsero, and thereby decreasing the rail distance between Denver and Salt Lake City to 570 miles. The 1200s were over-

# Rio Grande Territory

Despite its modest size among western railroads, the D&RGW operated its lines through regions having quite diverse characteristics, both geologic and geographic in nature. This diversity determined the locations of the various lines and branches, as well as the traffic and motive power needed to move it. It should not be too surprising to find that most Rio Grande locomotives were designed for a specific service over a particular route or branch, and that they were rarely operated elsewhere. This situation was most evident for freight trains, but passenger trains engines were operated over the railroad's entire mainline and principal branches. One peculiar by-product of these motive-power assignments is the scarcity of photos showing the locomotives on the road pulling trains, where access by highway was limited. One such region was eastern Utah between Helper and Grand Junction, CO, the habitat of the ten monstrous 3-cylinder 4-8-2s (1600-1609). So remote was the Colorado River east of the Utah-Colorado boundary that there are no known photos of a fairly common sight-a 1600 double-heading with a 4-6+6-4.

After World War II, as diesel-electric units replaced steam power, locomotives assigned west of Grand Junction gravitated toward Salt Lake City for scrapping. Those working east of Grand Junction went to the Pueblo for dismantling. The transition produced some unusual sights when engines were relocated to handle traffic surges. One ex-D&SL 2-6+6-0 and a companion 2-8-2 were found in Salt Lake City, and a 3500 was seen in Alamosa, accompanied by a D&SL Mallet and one of the big 3600-series 2-8+8-2s. Several 4-6+6-4s worked out of Pueblo to Denver, Minturn and La Veta. The 3600s were retained as helpers at Tabernash, Denver, and Minturn and they hauled freight trains between Denver and Alamosa. The 1500s, which had hauled mainline freight trains, were used on the 2-car passenger train between Denver and Craig; and 1700s, which had pulled the Scenic Limited, worked on Denver-Pueblo local freight trains. Perhaps the biggest surprise was the 1403, a 2-10-2, which had come over Tennessee Pass from Utah to Pueblo, thence over Wagon Creek Pass to Alamosa. How that big engine managed to negotiate the labyrinth of sharp curves between La Veta and Ft. Garland, without derailing, was a most remarkable feat. Only a few of these unusual assignments were recorded on film and they ended when diesel-electric units arrived.

hauled by the installation of mechanical stokers, firebox syphons and powered reverse, and were re-assigned to passenger service over this new route. Then, as train lengths increased during World War II, they were superseded by powerful 4-8-4s. However, their careers were not yet over. They worked on secondary-line runs: Denver and Craig, Denver and Montrose, Denver and Alamosa, Salt Lake City and Marysvale. About half of these 2-8-2s were scrapped in 1948, the others lingering until the end of Rio Grande steam power in 1956, when the 1207 was scrapped. The consist of the "Pacific" and "Atlantic" expresses had become so long that the 4-6-0s could not maintain the schedules. The remedy for this situation was a 4-6-2 having the same size driving wheels (67 in.) as the 4-6-0 and the boiler from the 2-8-2. Baldwin delivered six of them, numbered 1001-1006, in 1913. Compared with the 4-6-0s, they had almost twice the firebox grate area and 50% more tractive effort. Double-heading was eliminated, except for the steep grades of Soldier Summit and Tennessee Pass. After their replacement by huge 4-8-2s in 1922, they hauled secondary mainline trains, and after World War II they displaced 4-6-0s on branches to Craig, Montrose and Alamosa. All of them were scrapped between 1949 and 1953, when diesel-displaced larger engines took over their runs.

As mainline traffic increased the D&RG's original profile was becoming an operational nightmare. Westbound trains ascended a 1.4% grade to Tennessee Pass, while eastbound trains from Glenwood Springs encountered 1.6% grades and a 21-mile 3% climb to the summit. In Utah, things were no better; the westbound gradient from Helper was 2-2.4%, and from Thistle eastward the grade was

*Six new 4-6-2s, like the 1001, replaced ten compound-expansion 4-6-0s on the Atlantic Coast and the Pacific Coast Limiteds between Denver and Salt Lake City. This view may have shown the first trip departing Denver's Union Depot in 1913. LeMC*

2% plus seven miles of 4%. Double and triple heading was becoming increasingly uneconomical; the problem was attacked in two ways: gradient reduction and larger locomotives. Accordingly, in 1913 the 4% segment was replaced with a huge double-horseshoe relocation fourteen miles of 2% grade. No such relocation was possible on Tennessee Pass, due to the unfavorable terrain.

Because there was no practical way to reduce the gradients over Tennessee Pass and Soldier Summit the D&RG decided to purchase much more powerful locomotives which could haul freight trains unassisted between Glenwood Springs and Salida, and between Thistle and Helper. Also, they could be utilized as helpers between Minturn and Tennessee Pass and between Helper and Soldier Summit. These locomotives, sixteen of them numbered 1050-1075, were among the earliest and heaviest 2-8+8-2 Mallets. Weighing 458,000 pounds, they had twice the zero-speed tractive effort of the 2-8-0s—95000 lbs.—and nearly twice the grate area—80 sq. ft. They possessed enormous low-pressure

cylinders—40 in.—and their boilers had superheaters, a necessity to prevent condensation in such huge cylinders. As was customary with American Locomotive Company's design, the low-pressure cylinders were equipped with slide-valves and the high-pressure ones with piston-valves; and an inside-bearing trailing truck supported the rear of the firebox. The 57-inch drivers were the same as those of the 2-8-0s, making them the operational equivalent of two smaller engines. The 96/106-in. diameter boiler was among the

*Unlike other railroads which acquired 2-6+6-2 articulated locomotives for mainline service, the Rio Grande utilized its eight Mallet-compounds on branches in Utah which originated enormous tonnages of copper and precious metal ores and coal. No. 1055 was working at Bingham, UT at the great open-pit copper deposit, whence it would take a train of ore to the concentrators and smelters west of Salt Lake City. These were the last Rio Grande engines to use saturated steam, which flowed from the steam dome through an outside pipe to the high-pressure cylinders. REC*

largest built for a steam locomotive.

This fleet of sixteen 2-8+8-2s was numerically second only to that of the Southern Pacific, and that position was maintained until 1920, when the Norfolk & Western greatly expanded its roster of them. They arrived just in time to carry the burden of World War I traffic, and by 1923 replacements were needed to move the coal tonnage in Utah. Thereafter, they worked almost exclusively in Colorado on all mainlines and major branches. Just prior to World War II, they were given piston-valve cylinders and firebox syphons, which increased their tractive effort in the 10-30 mph range. During the war six of them were provided with new boilers, a program which was halted when diesel-electric units began to arrive. Scrapping commenced in 1944, but most of them remained active until 1950-1952.

World War I created an enormous increase in the demand for coal which was mined near Trinidad, CO. and delivered to Denver or to the Colorado Fuel & Iron Company's iron and steel works south of Pueblo. The D&RG was unable to handle the immense tonnages involved with its existing motive power; so, in 1916 it obtained ten ponderous 2-10-2s from the American Locomotive Co. Weighing 429,000 lbs., they were the heaviest non-articulated engines on earth, and could exert an 81000-lb. tractive effort. Their boilers were almost as big as those of the recent Mallet 2-8+8-2s, and their driving wheels were the same size as those of the 2-8-2s. They were the only Rio Grande engines to have been equipped with cylindrical tenders (excepting a few older 2-8-0s) as well as the Cole-type trailing truck. The driving axle loads were exceptionally heavy 70000-72000 lbs.-at that time, and much greater than the 54000 lbs. loading of the 2-8+8-2 Mallets. The profile northward from Trinidad was not demanding, but north of Pueblo there was a 1.4 maximum gradient up to Palmer Lake. After 1922 a major change in motive power assignments sent these locomotives to work between Helper and Provo, UT and there they remained until their retirement in 1952-1955. Modifications included firebox syphons, Elesco feedwater heaters (mounted below the smokebox),

The 1209 was assisting 2-8+8-2 No. 3414 with a long freight train departing Denver over the Moffat Tunnel route. The helper would turn at East Portan and return to Denver. HKVC

12-wheel tenders (removed from ex-Norfolk & Western 2-8+8-2s), and the installation of over-fire air-jets to prevent excessive smoke.

Even though the Rio Grande needed more locomotives to move the freight and passenger traffic generated by World War I, no more were obtained until 1922, after the railroad had been financially reorganized. What had transpired as a bizarre sequence of events in which the D&RG lost its investment in the Western Pacific, and then became a debtor to hostile financial manipulators. The railroad's precarious financial and physical condition was to continue until a final reorganization in 1947. During this 6-year period of acute monetary stringency and under-maintained track the Rio Grande's mechanical department designers went right ahead, planning even bigger, heavier and more powerful locomotives. One would have thought that they were working for the "Virginian of the Rockies", with unlimited funds for locomotives and track. That state of affairs manifested itself during the subsequent two decades until the arrival of the railroad's last new steam power. It has been said that the motive power people "ran the Rio Grande", and history

*The immense 2-10-2s were delivered at Denver, where they were set up, then broken in on trial runs to Sedalia, CO. They were the first Rio Grande locomotives having the Cole-type trailing truck, and the only ones with Baker valve-gear. These engines retained their small cylindrical tenders during thirty years of service because their runs were relatively short. (OCP).*

When they were constructed in 1913, the huge 2-8+8-2s were the D&RG's first "super-power" engines, ranking second only to the Virginian's 2-8+8-2s built a year earlier. One of them replaced a pair of 2-8-0s as mainline helpers. Resplendent in shiny new paint, the 1075 has just rolled out of American's erecting shop in Schenectady, NY, and was awaiting its long journey to Denver. A pair of 4-6-0s could take the eastbound Scenic Limited upgrade from Glenwood Springs to Minturn, but to ascend the northern approach to Tennessee Pass one of the big articulated Mallets was required, augmenting the 58000 pounds of tractive effort of the small engines by 96000 pounds. (ALC, 1075; CVC, 1061).

After hauling mainline freight trains for a decade, the fourteen 2-8-2s were superseded by more powerful 4-8-2s and thereafter worked in local freight service. Then, when the Dotsero Cutoff was completed in 1934, some of them were equipped with smoke deflectors for use over the D&SL, pulling passenger trains as far as Bond. The 1205 shows its cosmetic embellishments at Denver in 1939. HKVC.

seems to support that contention. This passion for large, heavy and powerful locomotives was not without adequate justification: the Rio Grande's extremely difficult profile. Between Denver and Pueblo, there was a ridge flanked by 1.4% gradients. Northwestward from Pueblo the track followed the Arkansas River on long 1.2-1.4% gradients to Tennessee Pass at 10240 ft. elevation. North of the summit the gradient was 3%, then 1.6% and 1% to Grand Junction on the Colorado River. Between the Colorado and Green Rivers was a low summit, then an ascent of the Wasatch Mountains on 2-2.4% gradients to Soldier Summit. On its western slope, the gradient was 2%, thence 1% into Salt Lake City. Three percent gradients were needed to surmount Wagon Creek Pass between La Veta and Alamosa, CO. These lines required maximum low-speed drawbar-pull, as well as maximum horsepower at operating speeds, a combination which required large boilers and fireboxes, and heavy driving axle loads.

| Year | Road Numbers | Wheel Arrangement | Driver | Weight of Engine | Tractive Effort | Type | Builder |
|------|--------------|-------------------|--------|------------------|-----------------|------|---------|
| 1910 | 1050-1057 | 2-6+6-2 | 57 | 340,000 | 62000 | compound articulated | ALC |
| 1912 | 1200-1213 | 2-8-2 | 63 | 276,000 | 59000 | | BLW |
| 1912 | 1001-1006 | 4-6-2 | 67 | 261,000 | 45000 | | BLW |
| 1913 | 1060-1075 | 2-8+8-2 | 57 | 458,000 | 95000 | compound articulated | ALC |
| 1916 | 1250-1259 | 2-10-2 | 63 | 429,000 | 81000 | cylindrical tenders | ALC |

Both groups of articulateds were equipped with slide-valves on the front cylinders and piston-valves on the rear cylinders. The 2-6+6-2s did not have superheaters originally.

# *Superpower in the Rockies* 1922-1927

The financial catastrophes which engulfed the Rio Grande during the 1915-1924 decade were so attractive to historians that they overlooked the remarkable accomplishments of the railroad's motive power department. The D&RG/D&RGW competed with the giants of the industry—Union Pacific, Santa Fe, and the Southern Pacific—whose huge rosters of locomotives drew the attention of both private and industrial publications. Even the financial manuals—Moody's and Poor's—did little more than to count the locomotives and total their tractive efforts. Baldwin Locomotives magazine published (1929) a detailed article about the operations of the Rio Grande's trains and locomotive assignments, but said almost nothing about the design and capabilities of the railroad's superlative newer locomotives. Unlike Baldwin, American Locomotive did not publish an in-house journal which extolled the accomplishments of the

*The 1502, at Denver in 1939, appeared very much as it had when delivered. (HKVC)*

company's locomotives. Instead, it relied on considerable advertising in various editions of the Locomotive Cyclopedia. Fortunately, photos, erection drawings and specifications were preserved in that publication, and these have been used extensively in this account.

The D&RG somehow managed to handle the traffic associated with World War-I without any additional motive power. Meanwhile, it had undergone a bankruptcy and a financial reorganization, emerging in 1921 as the Denver & Rio Grande Western. In the following year the railroad again failed financially, and the court became its new manager. Changes were made immediately; new locomotives were ordered, and track improvements were commenced. The first ten engines were the biggest and heaviest constructed thus far. Rio Grande and American designers began with the huge boiler from the 2-10-2s, and provided it with a slightly smaller firebox. They retained the 63-inch drivers, and reduced the maximum axle-load to 68000 lbs. The engine weighed 377,000 lbs. and could exert a 67000-lb. tractive effort, both quantities having been greater than those of any existing 4-8-2. Strangely, the trade press ignored these superb locomotives completely, though many lesser locomotives of larger railroads were documented with erection drawings and specifications.

These powerful locomotives were needed to pull the Scenic Limited which had become so long that the 4-6-2s required double-heading with 4-6-0s.

Rio Grande and American Locomotive Company staffs designed the 1500s with the largest boiler ever mounted on a 4-8-2 chassis. They used the boiler from the 2-10-2—96 inches diameter—but reduced the firebox grate area 10%. The boiler for the Pennsylvania's 4-8-2 would have fit inside it with 12 inches clearance all around, and they were just as tall as the Union Pacific's gigantic 4-12-2s. Other innovations included a cast-frame Delta-type trailing truck and a tender, holding 14000 gallons and 26 tons, which rode on 6-wheel trucks.

In 1950, the 1503 and 1513 were struggling uphill at Greenland, CO, with a southbound freight train. (RWA)

The operating department soon discovered that these engine were far superior to the 2-8-2s for mainline freight service; so 20 more were purchased during 1923 from American Locomotive. Engines 1511-1520 were equipped with trailing-truck boosters, one of the earliest applications of that device, and the first on a 4-8-2. Those numbered 1501-1510 and 1521-1530 did not have the booster, which added 12000 lbs. to the tractive effort at very low speeds. The total drawbar-pull of these locomotives was surpassed only by 4-8-2s of the DL&W, IC and SL-SF. The 1511-1520, with boosters, worked over the hump between Denver and Pueblo, hauling both passenger and freight trains, and the other twenty engines worked over Tennessee Pass as far as Grand Junction. It was not recognized at the time, but these were truly the first heavy duty dual-service locomotives on the continent. They performed so satisfactorily that the first ones were not retired until 1949, and several ran on the Alamosa line and the Craig branch until 1955, a year prior to the end of steam power on the D&RGW.

While American's factory in Dunkirk, NY, was erecting the big 4-8-2s, the Richmond, VA, plant was building ten 2-8+8-2s, which were facsimiles of 106 USRA engines delivered to coal-hauling eastern railroads at the end of World War I. The D&RGW and Northern Pacific were the only western railroads to acquire these powerful Mallets, but the Rio Grande used them in over-the-road service while the NP assigned its four engines to slow speed helper duties. These new articulateds were much larger, heavier and more powerful than the earlier ones. The boiler had a 98 in. diameter and a 240-psi pressure, and the firebox and grate area were larger also. Weighing 532,000 pounds with an axle loading of 61000 lbs., the engine could exert a 107,000-lb. tractive effort. Their arrival resulted in a major relocation of the railroad's larger locomotives. The 3500-

3509 worked between Helper and Thistle, over Soldier Summit, replacing the older Mallets, which were sent to Colorado. The 2-10-2s were moved to Utah, where they remained. These ten engines spent their entire careers pulling and pushing heavy trains up to Soldier Summit until their gradual retirement between 1947 and 1951.

The D&RGW's next new locomotives involved a peculiar series of events. The railroad wanted a passenger service engine with the same zero-speed drawbar-pull as the booster-equipped 4-8-2s, but with larger drivers to reduce track damage at higher speeds. It appears that the American Locomotive Company suggested a 3-cylinder configuration, which it had been promoting since 1922. It had built 4-8-2s for the Lehigh Valley, Lackawanna, and New Haven, 4-10-2s for the Southern Pacific, and 4-12-2s for the UP. Driver diameter was increased to 67 in., and the boiler diameter decreased by the same amount to reduce total weight, which was still an incredible 419,000 lbs., a figure which was barely surpassed by a few 4-8-2s constructed during World War II. Enlarged to accommodate 95 sq. ft. of grate area, the immense firebox imposed a 61000 lb. load on the trailing axle, which would have been heavier had not the stoker engine been placed on the tender. Rated drawbar-pull was 75000 lbs., but the tonnage-rating was 78000 lbs., easily attained by the more uniform torque of the three cylinders. Driving axle loads were a track-crushing 73000 lbs.; due partly to the feedwater heaters. These powerful engines were much too heavy for the Rio Grande's deteriorated track, and the maintenance gangs could not replace 90-pound rail rapidly enough with barely adequate 100-pound rail.

It was evident that American had been the intended builder of the engines, but Baldwin obtained the order, despite its lack of experience with 3-cylinder construction, probably because a "confidential" discount had been offered, a not uncommon

No. 1505 was double-heading with 4-8-4 No. 1804 on the westbound Exposition Flyer near Tolland, CO., in 1941. HRG/CRM

practice. Baldwin, however, could not use the 2-lever Gresley valve-gear for the middle cylinder because American held the exclusive license; so, a second Walschaerts mechanism was added to the right side of the engine to actuate the middle valve. This awkward arrangement appears to have been satisfactory during almost three decades of service.

Numbered 1600-1609, these super-power 4-8-2s were assigned to the "Scenic Limited" between Denver and Salt Lake City, thereby releasing the ten-booster-equipped 1511-1520 4-8-2s for freight service between Salida and Glenwood Springs. After three years of track-destruction the railroad's management felt that these behemoths were better suited to hauling freight trains at lower speeds, and they were put to work between Grand Junction and Helper, where they remained until their retirement.

By 1926, the D&RGW was operating a fleet of formidable locomotives in mainline service—forty 4-8-2s, ten 2-10-2s, and 26 2-8+8-2s. Its adjacent competitors—Santa Fe and Union Pacific—were employing smaller 4-8-2s and 2-10-2s, as was the Southern Pacific. The SP had some ancient 2-8+8-2s, and the UP used recent 2-8+8-0s. The Rio Grande was right up front with the giants of the industry. This excellent motive power situation was marred, however, by excessive double-heading caused by the Rio Grande's difficult profile in Colorado. The remedy appeared to be a single-expansion 2-8+8-2 having a steam production of at least 100,000 lbs. per hour. American Locomotive's designers copied the propulsion machinery of the 1923 Baldwin-built Great Northern's 2-8+8-2, but there was no existing boiler/firebox to generate sufficient steam. So, they designed one having a grate area of 137 sq. ft. and 240 psi. steam pressure. This enormous boiler was ten inches larger in diameter than that of the

15

1600s, and three thermic siphons were installed in its firebox to increase water circulation and steam generation. When completed, the engine alone weighed 650,000 lbs. with driving axle loads of 69000-71000 lbs. Initially, the maximum cutoff was limited to prevent slipping at 125,000 lbs. tractive effort, but this precaution was found unnecessary, and the rated tractive effort became 131,000 lbs.

American erected ten of the gigantic locomotives, numbered 3600-3609, during 1927 at Dunkirk. They were the last articulateds produced at that plant before it closed in 1929. The bill for the locomotives came to $121,405 each, which was a good investment because they reduced the operating costs from 72 cents to 58 cents per 1000 gross ton-miles, not accounting for extra track maintenance. Somewhere in this period the D&RGW's parody among employees changed from "Dilapidated and Rapidly Getting Worse" to "Dangerous..." They were the world's most powerful steam locomotives, and they retained the title until 1931, when Baldwin delivered some more potent 2-8+8-2s to the Western Pacific.

Their original assignment was the mainline between Salida and Grand Junction, through helpers were needed on the 3% grade from Minturn to Tennessee Pass. Elsewhere on the mainline in Colorado forty big boilered 4-8-2s supplemented the mighty articulateds, while in Utah 4-8-2s, 2-10-2s and USRA-standard 2-8+8-2s handled the traffic. It was in this era that "super-power" was the buzzword of the railroad

industry; and the Rio Grande had been at the head of the movement since the acquisition of its first 4-8-2s in 1922. By 1927, it was truly a super-power railroad.

(Note) The Pennsylvania's 2-8+8-0 and the Virginian's 2-10+10-2 had greater tractive effort at very low speeds, but their smaller fireboxes limited their drawbar-horsepower at 10-20 mph. The Northern Pacific's 2-8+8-4, built by American in 1928, used the 3600's boiler and propulsion machinery with a much larger firebox. However, the NP used a very poor grade of coal, and consequently it could not attain the horsepower developed by the D&RGW's 3600s.

| Year | Road Numbers | Wheel Arrangement | Driver Diameter | Weight of Engine | Tractive Effort | Type | Builder |
|------|------|------|------|------|------|------|------|
| 1922 | 1501-1510 | 4-8-2 | 63 | 376,000 | 67000 | | ALC |
| 1923 | 1511-1520 | 4-8-2 | 63 | 384,000 | 78000 | (TT Booster) | ALC |
| 1923 | 3500-3509 | 2-8+8-2 | 57 | 532,000 | 107000 | compound articulated | ALC |
| 1923 | 1521-1530 | 4-8-2 | 63 | 376,000 | 67000 | | ALC |
| 1926 | 1600-1609 | | | | | | |
| 1927 | 3600-3609 | 2-8+8-2 | 63 | 650,000 | 125000 | (limited cutoff-single expansion articulated | ALC |

1600-1604 had Worthington feedwater heaters; 1605-1609 used Elesco. All of the 4-8-2s had cast frame (Delta) trailing trucks. All of the 2-8+8-2s had fabricated frame (Cole) trailing trucks. The 3600s had outside-bearing leading trucks.

The handiwork of the Salt Lake City shops is evident in this 1949 portrait of 1509—smoke deflector, sloped-front cab and overfire air openings to reduce smoke. (HKVC)

No. 1707 was double-heading with Union Pacific 4-6+6-4 No. 3959 at Palmer Lake in 1949 when the UP's mainline across Wyoming was blocked by snowdrifts. *OCP*

# *More Superpower*

# 1928-1938

3

**B**y the end of 1926 the D&RGW possessed a most impressive roster of steam locomotives, particularly when one considers its relatively small mileage. Most of its mainline engines were unequaled for size, weight or power. Its 40 huge dual service 4-8-2s was exceeded numerically by those of the Union Pacific (50) and Santa Fe (51), and the Rio Grande engines were more powerful. The UP's heavy freight locomotives were 65 2-8+8-0s; the D&RGW employed 26 compound-expansion 2-8+8-2s and 10 single-expansion 2-8+8-2s, which were the largest and most powerful steam engines on earth. Both the Santa Fe and Union Pacific relied on 2-10-2s for freight service, but the Rio Grande preferred the faster 4-8-2, and assigned its ten 2-10-2s to slow speed coal hauling.

Unfortunately, however, the ten 1600s and ten 3600s with their enormous axle loads were being operated at 40 mph and they were gradually destroying the railroad's less-than-substantial track structure. This serious situation was solved in 1929 by the purchase of fourteen Baldwin 4-8-4s, numbered 1700-1713. Once again, the D&RGW was ahead of its competitors; the UP wasn't even considering such locomotives and the SF had just begun to receive its first ones of that wheel arrangement. Also, this acquisition was an example of Baldwin's obtaining an order for engines which had been designed for construction by American. These engines were dimensional duplicates of the 4-8-4s which American was building for the Lackawanna, though embodying some variations-slab frames, Elesco feedwater heater and two compound air pumps. Having 70-inch drivers and axle load of only 63,000 lbs., they were able to haul passenger trains at higher speeds than any of the 4-8-2s.

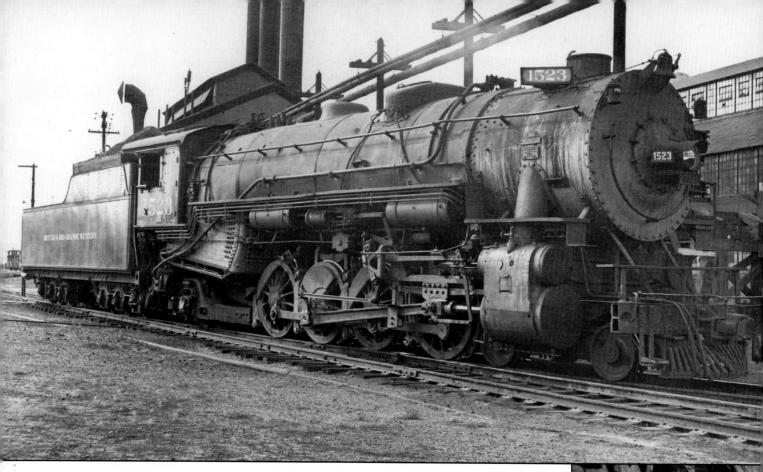

*A Loco Valve Pilot had been installed on the 1523 seen at Salida in 1942, a junction with the D&RGW's narrow gauge system.  HKVC*

The displaced 1500s remained in freight service in Colorado, but the 1600s were transferred to the Grand Junction-Helper segment where they handled freight consists at lower speeds.

Despite their track wrecking propensities, the railroad appeared to have been satisfied with the tonnage hauling abilities of the big single-expansion 2-8+8-2s. One of them was the practical equivalent of a 2-8-0 double-heading with a 4-8-2, and, moreover, they could run faster. Yet, they did display some objectionable aspects:  they smoked prodigiously with little provocation, and when they worked hard at low speeds 25% of the coal went from stoker jets to the stack without yielding much heat of combustion. Nevertheless the Rio Grande bought ten more of them, incorporating an improved boiler and superheater, from American in 1930. At this point in time the Rio Grande must have resembled the Virginian railway in the East. Powerful 2-8+8-2s, three to a train, took freight trains

up the 3% grade on the northern side of Tennessee Pass in Colorado, while two helped a 2-10-2 ascend the 2.2% grade east of Soldier Summit in Utah. Passenger trains, pulled by a 4-8-4, needed one of the articulateds to climb the steep terrain. And, the 3% grades on both flanks of Wagon Creek Pass, between La Veta and Alamosa, required them also. Then there were the eight 2-6+6-2s, which brought coal out of the winding canyons to the yard at Helper, Utah. This concentration of motive power—108 locomotives—most of which were unsur-

So satisfactory were its big 4-8-2s that the D&RGW bought twenty more a year later, the first ten of which were equipped with a trailing-truck booster, a very easy installation of this new drawbar-pull enhancement. At that time there wasn't any comparable 4-8-2, and they were barely surpassed by later locomotives, which probably accounts for their remarkable longevity. The 1511, brand new, was leading the eastbound Scenic Limited over newly relocated track through Granite Canyon in Colorado. Waiting for the conductor's highball, No. 1516 was ready to depart Salida in 1949 with a train of limestone consigned to the steel mill at Minnequa, CO. The westbound Scenic Limited was being escorted down the 3.3% grade in Eagle River Canyon by No. 1527, which was using the water-brake to control the train's speed. Note the absence of brakeshoe smoke. (RRA, 1511; HKVC, 1516, RRA, 1527).

*The USRA-standard 2-8+8-2 had been designed for coal hauling railroads in the eastern U. S.A.; hence, the D&RGW was unique in operating ten of them over Soldier Summit between Provo and Helper, UT, where the maximum gradients were 2% eastward and 2.4% westward. Because loaded coal trains moved westward from Helper, a 2-10-2 would be placed at the head end, with a pair of 3500s pushing at the rear. Only one 2-8+8-2 was needed to bring the empty cars back over the hill. Also, they worked as head-end helpers for passenger and merchandise trains.* Lower Right: *In a typical scene at Castle Gate, UT, in 1939, the 3501 and 3503 were just commencing their labors behind a solid coal consist.* Top Right: *A bit earlier the same engine at Helper was awaiting another trip over the hill.* Above: *Repairs and periodic inspections were done at the shops in Salt Lake City, which accounts for the presence of No. 3508 there in 1950. Lacking over-fire air inlets, these articulateds were not allowed to run regularly into Salt Lake City. (OCP, 3501/3503; RWA, 3506; HKVC, 3506, 3508).*

passed in size or power, was without parallel in the nation west of the Mississippi River.

One might question the Rio Grande's wisdom in acquiring the last group of 2-8+8-2s on the eve of the Great Business Depression, but other elements beyond such considerations as operating costs or ton-miles per-hour train. To comprehend this aspect, some geographical history is needed. Dotsero, at the junction of the Eagle and Colorado rivers, was 342 miles from Denver via Pueblo and Salida. Yet it was only 167 miles by another route through the Moffat Tunnel which had been completed in 1928, and which was being used by the Denver and Salt Lake railway. Between Orestod, on the D&SL 128 miles from Denver, was an easy 41-mile grade along the Colorado River. This route was known to early railroad surveyors, but it was of little utility until the Moffat Tunnel

was completed. The "Dotsero Cutoff" was completed in 1934 and an engine terminal was established at Bond, a mile west of the actual junction. This was needed because of the D&SL's track and structures could not support the big 3600s, and the lighter 3400s ran over the D&SL until 1936, when the rehabilitation program was completed. Though it was shorter, the Moffat Tunnel route presented some difficult operating conditions. The 50-mile climb from Denver was almost all on a 2% gradient, with 10-12° curves and 29 tunnels. Between Orestod and the 6-mile summit tunnel there were nine short ones, plus a 15°curve and 11 miles of 2% gradient east of the helper terminal at Tabernash. The Rio Grande assigned some of the 3400-series Mallets between Denver and Bond, replacing them with the more powerful 3600s. Passenger service between Denver and Grand Junction commenced in 1935, the trains

having been pulled by 2-8-2s.

Even though the D&RGW had established a new and shorter route through the mountains, it was unable to avoid financial collapse in 1935, and the railroad was placed in a locally managed trusteeship. Almost immediately the two trustees were confronted with a motive power problem imposed by its closest competitors. In 1935, the UP acquired 20 big 4-8-4s, and in 1936 it bought 15 4-6+6-4s, the first of that new wheel arrangement. In the following year, the AT&SF added 11 larger 4-8-4s to its

fleet. Then in 1938, the Santa Fe purchased ten gigantic 2-10-4s having 74-inch drivers. To counter these threats of freight traffic diversion, the Rio Grande acquired five new 4-8-4s (1800-1804) and ten enormous 4-6+6-4s from Baldwin in 1937 and 1938.

Weighing 479,000 lbs. and having a 92-inch boiler diameter, the D&RGW's new 4-8-4s were larger than those of its two competitors. Having a rated tractive effort of 68000 lbs., augmented by 6000 lbs. due to a full installation of roller bearings, they could take the *Scenic Limited* up any main-

At Rio, UT in 1949, the 3506 was pushing empties eastward. RWA

line grade between Denver and Salt Lake City without a helper, excepting only the northern side of Tennessee Pass, and their 73-inch drivers enabled them to run at 80 mph without damaging the track, despite their 70000-lbs. axle loading.

After the big 3600s began operating over the Moffat Tunnel route, the D&RGW faced a perplexing problem between Grand Junction and Salt Lake City. The 3600s were too slow; the 3500s were slower and older; the 1600s were too small and not very new; and the 1400s were both old and sluggish. What the railroad needed was a locomotive with the power of a 3600, the drivers of a 1700, and the tractive effort of a 3500. Baldwin was given an order for ten locomotives incorporating all of these specifications—a 4-6+6-4 having an axle load of 73000 lbs.—although that company had previously built only lighter 2-6+6-4s. Moreover, the engine was bigger than those which American had delivered to the Union Pacific and the Northern Pacific. Its grate area was the same as that of the 2-8+8-2s—137 sq. ft.—which enabled it to develop 6000 drawbar-horsepower, a figure surpassed by only the Norfolk & Western 2-6+6-4, the Chesapeake & Ohio 2-6+6-6, the Union Pacific 4-8+8-4, and possibly the Northern Pacific's oil-fired 4-6+6-4s. The installation of roller-bearings on all engine and tender axles added about 10000 lbs. to the 105,000 lbs. tractive effort, thus eliminating helpers except for maximum tonnage trains over Soldier Summit.

After their displacement by the more powerful 1800s, the 1700s worked on the branches to Ogden, Montrose and Alamosa, then also on the Scenic Limited until after World War II. They were used as passenger train helpers to the Moffat Tunnel, and in their final days pulled the ski train between Denver and Winter Park. The first ones were scrapped in 1950, but three of them made their last runs in 1955. The 1800s, due to their greater tractive effort and horsepower, were utilized on the Moffat Tunnel line between Denver and Grand Junction during World War II, then were transferred to the Royal Gorge route when diesel-electric motive power displaced them. The first one was retired in 1953, and all of them were out of service by 1955. The massive 3600s, which had hauled mainline freight trains over both routes, were first displaced from the Moffat Tunnel line by diesel-electric units, and subsequently lost their head-end positions between Pueblo and Salt Lake City, though retaining their status between Denver and Alamosa. Thereafter, they became helpers in Utah, on Tennessee Pass, and on both sides of the Moffat Tunnel Line. Their final refuge was Tabernash, where the 3609, 3612 and 3619 worked until October 1956, when mainline steam operations were concluded. The story of the 3700s will be found in the next chapter, because there were three groups of 4-6+6-4s, only one of which has been accounted for thus far.

| Year | Road Numbers | Wheel Arrangement | Driver | Weight of Engine | Tractive Effort | Type | Builder |
|------|------|------|------|------|------|------|------|
| 1929 | 1700-1713 | 4-8-4 | 70 | 418,000 | 64000 | | BLW |
| 1930 | 3610-3619 | 2-8+8-2 | 63 | 665,000 | 132000 | | ALC |
| 1937 | 1800-1804 | 4-8-4 | 73 | 479,000 | 68000 + 6000RB | | BLW |
| 1938 | 3700-3709 | 4-6+6-4 | 70 | 642,000 | 105,000 + 10000RB | | BLW |

1700s, 1800s and 3700s were built by Baldwin. 3600s were built by American.
1800s and 3700s had enclosed cabs and roller bearings on all engine and tender axles. 3600s and 3700s had single-expansion cylinders. 1800s and 3700s had integrally cast machinery beds. 1700s and 3600s had slab type frames.

Believe it or not—the 1600s basic dimensions were the same as those of the Union Pacific's monstrous 4-12-2s: boiler diameter, centerline height and driving wheel size. The 4-8-2s appeared less formidable because their air pumps were placed just ahead of the firebox flanks, and an extra Walschaerts valve-gear on the right side replaced the double-lever mechanism which would have been installed ahead of the cylinders. The 1600 posed for its official portrait at the Burnham roundhouse when it was delivered, then at Salida a year later it was being serviced for a trip over Tennessee Pass to Grand Junction. (RRA, Burnham; RHKC, Salida).

After an overnight trip across the Utah desert from Helper, the 1600 leads 4-6+6-4 No. 3706 into the yards at Grand Junction. The doubled valve-gear on the right side can be seen in this 1938 view of the 1600 at Grand Junction. The raised headlight, flat smokebox door and slanted-front cab were "hall-marks" of the Salt Lake City shops which modified locomotives without bothering to inform officials in Denver. (OCP, 1600/3706; HKVC, 1600).

*Engines 1600-1604 were the only ones delivered with Worthington feedwater heaters; the 1605-1609 had Elesco heaters, which were also installed on the 1700s, 1800s, 3600s and 3700-3708. The 1606, at the head of an eastbound freight train, had stopped at Grand Valley, CO., in 1943 to replenish its water supply enroute to Glenwood Springs, where it would pick up a westbound consist for Grand Junction. The 1600s, though intended for the Scenic Limited between Denver and Salt Lake City, were soon superseded by faster 4-8-4s (1700s). The 1607, stopped in the Royal Gorge for the benefit of tourists, would become the last survivor of the group, making its final trip years later. (HKVC, 1606; RRA, 1607).*

# Riding the D&RGW's Locomotives

At the time of their delivery the Rio Grande's 1700s (1929) and 3600s (1927) represented state-of-the-art design and construction for heavy-duty mainline passenger and freight service. Though built by Baldwin, the 4-8-4s were dimensional duplicates of Lackawanna 4-8-4s erected by American at the same time, and differed principally in frame construction, air compressors and feedwater heater. The railroad assigned them to its passenger trains, whose consists could be twelve heavyweight cars, replacing 4-8-2s having much smaller driving wheels.

After World War II they worked on freight trains and as helpers for passenger trains until their retirement between 1950-1956. A few of them were modified with single-guide crossheads and firebox air-inlets, but otherwise they remained unchanged throughout their careers.

I rode on the 1710, pulling the 10-car Royal Gorge from Denver to Colorado Springs, 75 miles with a maximum gradient of 1.4%. The 110-minute schedule was "padded" to allow for late connections at Denver; so the 42 mph average speed with one intermediate stop was easily maintained. Between Denver and Wolhurst, where the gradient began to increase, the engine rode smoothly at 50-60 mph speeds, and from there to the summit at Palmer Lake the sustained 45 mph pace, which required maximum drawbar-horsepower, the 1710 ran remarkably smoothly. As the 1710 canted around a left-handed curve the distant horizon appeared to rise suddenly, and when it tilted through a right-hand curve, the horizon sank. One felt that the locomotive remained level, and that the terrain was twisting away beneath it. On the downhill side at 70 mph, restrained by the water-brake, the engine rode quite comfortably, without nosing or surging. Altogether, the trip was a rather pleasant experience aboard a very capable locomotive operated by a thoroughly competent engineer and fireman, who know how to make the 1710 perform smoothly and efficiently.

Our trip on the 3619 up to Tennessee Pass one night was an entirely different proposition, however. First of all, the 21-miles of double track between Minturn and the summit was more than twice as steep as that south of Denver—almost all of it inclined at 3%, the D&RGW's steepest mainline grade. (One coupler of an 85-foot Pullman car would be 31 inches higher that that on the opposite end!) Curvature was severe—8° to 12 1/2°— as well as continuous with few tangential places. Because the location of the line followed the canyon of the Eagle River, the scenery was just beyond one's outstretched arm on one side

or the other, and most of it was vertical. There were five tunnels on the uphill track, including one beneath the pass. At Pando, there was an "almost level" spot where engines could replenish their depleted water supply.

Eastbound passenger trains, pulled by a 4-8-4 would get a front end helper at Minturn for the 65-minute ascent; freight trains arrived behind one of the 3600s, and added one of two 2-8+8-2 helpers for their climb which consumed 2 to 2 1/2 hours, including the water stop at Pando. Helpers stationed at Minturn were combinations of 3400-series compound-expansion 2-8+8-2s rebuilt with new boilers and piston-valve cylinders, and the powerful single-expansion 3600-series 2-8+8-2s. When they were delivered by American in 1927, the 3600s were the most powerful steam locomotives on earth, capable of producing 5000 drawbar-horsepower. Ready-to- run, engine and tender weighed almost 1-million pounds.

C.R. McDonald was the No. 1 engineer between Salida and Grand Junction, he could have run the Royal Gorge every-other day, but he preferred to work in helper service at Minturn because it was more challenging and interesting. "You RAN a steam locomotive, but the diesels run you." We first met Mac at Minturn on a late August afternoon between trips up the hill. He took us into the roundhouse, climbed into the cab of the 3619, and began to tell us all about the engine. A few minutes later, a hostler joined us, ran the engine onto the turntable, thence to the coal chute to replenish fuel, water and sand. After the 3619 joined the 3600 and 3615 on the ready track, Mac invited us from supper in his home-away-from-home behind the roundhouse, and asked us to ride up the hill with him, leaving about 9 pm with a trainload of peaches.

Arriving an hour late, a quartet of GM F7 diesel units split its 56-car train in half, allowing the 3619 to fill the gap as mid-train helper. Meanwhile, the 3600 had backed down to pick-up the detached caboose, then help the 3619 re-assemble the whole consist, ready for the battle against gravity. The diesels would contribute 240,000 pounds of tractive effort, and the two ponderous articulateds would add another 260,000 pounds. As soon as the train had been inspected, the 3600's engineer blew its whistle, released the engine brakes, and opened the throttle. A few seconds later Mac repeated the sequence with the 3619, and two short blips for the diesels horn told us we were on our way to the highest mainline crossing of the North American Continental Divide.

The 3600s were very sure-footed machines, and though they produced excessive smoke without provocation, they did not exhibit uncontrolled driving wheel slipping which was typical of later single-expansion articulateds. At first, all that we could hear was the deafening hisses of wet steam escaping from the cool cylinders, and when these drain cocks were closed, we could hear the 3619's thunderous exhausts echoing from the canyon's walls as the train accelerated to normal running speed of 10-12 mph. Beneath the cab floor we could hear and feel the stoker engine and screw conveying coal for the tender into the cavernous firebox. The 1619's propulsion machinery was remarkably quiet, without the periodic clanking caused by worn mainrod bearings. The low rumble of the whole engine was just barely perceptible as the we plodded steadily upward.

South of Minturn only a couple of miles the canyon became so narrow that the uphill track had been located on the western side of the river, requiring the boring of three short tunnels at Belden. Just before entering them the engineer and fireman removed their heavy gloves, and gave one to each of us so that we could cover our mouth and nose during the suffocating passage. The cab became filled with a cloud of moist steam and pungent soft-coal smoke, so dense that we could barely see across it. When we emerged from the tunnels the bottom of the deep canyon was so dark that we could see nothing but the gage and dial illumination in otherwise totally black surroundings. The 3619 roared and rumbled past Red Cliff, a few specks of light clustered around the mouth of a tributary canyon; then we plunged back into the midnight realm as far a as Pando, where stopped for water.

Cooperation among the three engineers positioned the 3619's tender beside the water crane. The 3600 cut off and came up the siding to the other crane alongside the 3619. While the tenders were being filled, we climbed down to stretch our legs, and to gaze at the sky studded with a million stars so bright that we could barely distinguish the familiar constellations and the Milky Way, which we saw only occasionally in Denver. The atmosphere was so quiet

that we could hear a northbound freight train descending the grade long before we saw the headlight of its four-unit locomotive, whining in electrodynamic braking mode at 20 mph. It passed us just as we were departing Pando for the summit, 8 miles distant and 1,000 feet higher.

Having emerged from the tortuous canyon of the Eagel River, the single-track Deen tunnel, whose signals and switches were controlled from the Tennessee Pass depot, we were nearly 500 feet above the valley floor, invisible in the almost total darkness. Occasionally we could discern reflections from the diesel;s headlight and the marker lights on the caboose. Other wise, we could have been aboard a coal-fired, steam-propelled roaring and rumbling spacecraft headed for Mars. At Mitchell the track formed a gigantic S-curve in a broad open area immediately north of the pass, and we watched the headlight's beam enter the tunnel beneath it. Just before the 3619 went into the tunnel, Mac closed the throttle, allowing the forward half of the train to pull the drifting engine through without smoke, and likewise the 3600 was pulled through.

After stopping our train east of the tunnel, the diesel units pulled ahead, allowing our engine to slide over to the adjacent track, then backward through the wye. The 3600 pushed the two halfs of the train together, then followed us around the wye, and coupled to our tender in front of the depot. Having obtained a clearance card from the operator, Mac herded the two monsters back through the tunnel, thence downhill toward Minturn. He opened the

The 3600, assisted by another 2-8+8-2 pushing at the rear, was leaving Minturn with a train of iron ore enroute from Utah to Minnequa, CO. (NRM)

Within a year after having acquired the world's most powerful passenger-service steam locomotives (1600-1609), the D&RGW did the same for its freight trains when American delivered ten single-expansion 2-8+8-2s numbered 3600-3609. They possessed a zero-speed tractive effort 30% greater than previous 2-8+8-2s, as well as a 30% larger grate-area, which made them the operational equivalent of a booster-equipped 4-8-2 and a 2-8-0 helper. Top: The 3601, whose forward engine had been rebuilt with a cast steel bed and multiple-bearing crossheads, was taking on water before ascending the grade to Palmer Lake. Bottom: At Colorado Springs, just out of the shops at Burnham in 1946, the 3604 has received its unique enclosed cab and a complete repainting. Top Right: Note the new style lettering on the tender of 3609, resting between runs at Pueblo in 1948. (NRM, 3600; RHK, 3601; HKVC, 3604, 3609).

water-brake valve, cracked the throttle, opened the cylinder cocks and moved the cutoff control somewhat back of center. The 3619 would now roll downgrade at a steady 20 mph, restrained only by the water-brake. The 3600's engineer left the throttle slightly open to provide lubrication for the pistons.

Our return trip was quiet in comparison with the upgrade one. The engine's exhausts were almost inaudible, and the machinery produced a rhythmical clunking which reverberated from the rocky walls of the canyon. We had seen nothing in the canyon on the upward trip, but now the 3619's headlight illuminated the walls of the narrow gorge as we rounded the frequent curves, creating bizarre vistas known only to locomotive crews. The gentle rocking of the big locomotive as it undulated through the curves, combined with the muffled clanking of it's propulsion machinery, made it difficult for us to remain awake.

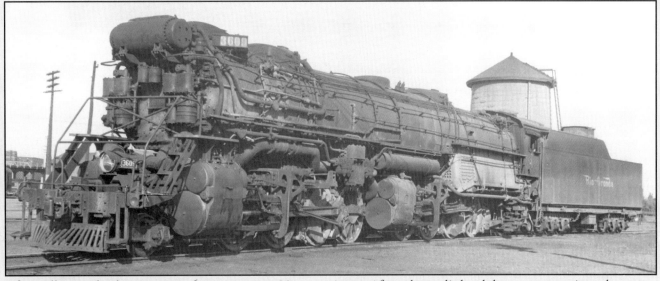

After all, we had arisen at 6 am, some 20 hours ago. Our somnolence ended abruptly with a loud BANG reinforced by its echo's from the canyon walls. Mac eased the engines to a halt beside red flare, and picked up the rear-end brakeman, who had been left behind by the freight train which had passed us at Pando more than two hours earlier. Under way once again, we had gone about a mile when the 3600's engineer applied the brakes. Tooting his whistle three times, he went back up the track to recover his own fireman who had gone back to protect us from the rear when we had stopped for a few minutes pre-vious. After these little delays we continued the descent into Minturn and slithered through the yard switches at 2:30 am.

At that hour Minturn's only hotel was closed; so we drove out of town a couple of miles and unrolled our sleeping bags in a small parking area, where we went to sleep immediately and dreamed about 3600s until we awoke. Then we discovered that our "dreams" were real, our site was at the top of a cut right beside the Rio Grande's tracks!

Thanks Mac, for a wonderful—and unfor-gettable—experience.

*Public timetable, Fall and Winter, 1939-1940. First timetable showing passenger service over the Moffat Tunel Route.*

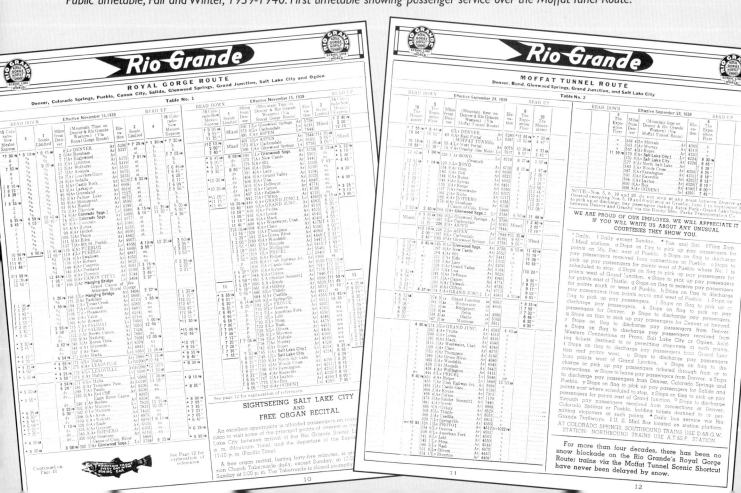

In the renumbering of 1924 the Rio Grande's 4-6-2s were given numbers 800-805. When the D&SL was absorbed in 1947, the 800s replaced 4-6-0s on the daily train between Denver and Craig. The 804, pulling an RPO car and a buffet-coach, wasn't working very hard as it climbed the 2% grade at Tolland, CO. Inset: At Denver, in 1946, it was awaiting repairs to its smoke deflector. (RWA, 804; HKVC, 805).

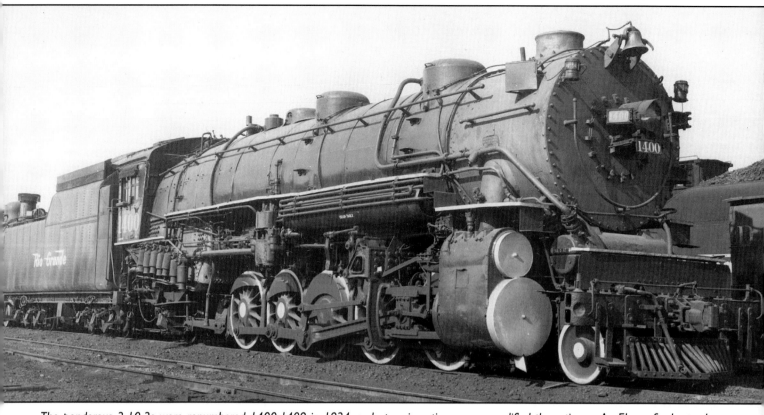

The ponderous 2-10-2s were renumbered 1400-1409 in 1924, and at various times were modified three times. An Elesco feedwater heater was installed beneath the smokebox in 1933, and ex-Norfolk & Western 12-wheel tenders from scrapped 2-8+8-2s replaced the small cylindrical ones. Overfire air-inlets were installed in 1946-1948, so that these locomotives could be operated into Salt Lake City, which prohibited excessive smoke. We don't know why the 1401 had been brought to Burnham Shops for a complete overhaul in the summer of 1948. The 1406 during the 1920s had a Worthington feedwater heater, which had been replaced by the Elesco model, and it still had its small tender in 1948. One year later at Salt Lake City, it had been overhauled and given a bigger, rectangular tender. All of the 2-10-2 cabs were changed to the sloping front, a characteristic of the Salt Lake City shops. (HKVC, 1401, 1406).

In 1949 the 1405, assisted by a 2-8+8-2 rear-end helper, was hauling a train of empty coal cars up the western side of Soldier Summit. RWA

Though the 4-8-2s possessed adequate power for the Rio Grande's passenger trains, their 63-inch drivers were too small for higher speed operations; consequently, in 1929 they were replaced by fourteen Baldwin 4-8-4s which were duplicates of those constructed by American for the Lackawanna railroad in the northeast. Differences were mainly their slab-type frames, Elesco feedwater heater and two compound air compressors. The 1701 had just arrived at the Burnham terminal after an overnight trip from Alamosa in 1950. During World War II, the westbound Exposition Flyer's 1800-series 4-8-4 would require the assistance of a 1700 on the 2% grade to the Moffat Tunnel. Here, the 1704 and 1801 had stopped for water at Pinecliff, CO. in 1943. Because the low-speed tractive effort of the 1700s was so much less than that of the 1600s, the motive power department doubted their ability to maintain schedules. Consequently, in a most unusual move, the railroad leased the locomotives for five years before accepting them.(HKVC, 1701; LEM, 1704/1801).

Westbound coal trains departing Helper, UT, for Soldier Summit needed one of the big 2-10-2s (No. 1404, top) on the headend and a pair of 3500 series 2-8+8-2s pushing at the rear (right) Despite the total tractive effort of 275,000 pounds the 27 mile ascent of the 2-2.4% grade consumed 2 ½ hours. Merchandise trains of lesser tonnages were given a pair of 2-10-2s like the 1404 and 1409, seen here just west of Castle Gate on a rare rainy day. (OCP 1404 (large), 1404, 1409 (small) RHK.

Twenty years after its arrival the 1710 was still pulling the Scenic Limited, leaving Salida for Denver, but its train was much shorter than it had been a decade earlier. RWA

In 1924 all of the oldest Mallets were renumbered. The 2-6+6-2s, number 1050-1057, became 3300-3307; the 2-8+8-2s, numbered 1060-1075, became 3400-3415. The 3301 and 3306, at Helper in 1940 and 1947, had been rebuilt during the 1930s with superheaters, which decreased coal and water consumption. The 3400, at Pueblo in 1940, and the 3406, at Salt Lake City in 1937, had been given smoke deflectors, as well as syphons in their firebox and combustion chamber to increase steam production. (HKVC, 3301, 3306, 3400 3406).

The 3610 was charging past the AT&SF depot at Palmer Lake, CO, the end of the long climb from Denver. In October, 1955, this could have been the locomotive's final run. Inset: The 3614, drifting to a stop at Salida in 1945, perfumed the atmosphere with voluminous clouds of soft coal smoke. (3610, RWA, 3614, LEM)

The D&RGW maintained its eminent motive-power status by adding ten more single-expansion 2-8+8-2s, numbered 3610-3619, in 1930. External differences were minor, but their boilers contained the more efficient Type-E superheater, which gave them more horsepower at operating speeds. During the severe business depression (1930-1936), the 3600s handled all first-class freight trains between Denver and Salt Lake City. Below: No. 3612, at Salt Lake City in 1950, had a single crosshead guide on the forward cylinders, indicating that the front engine had been rebuilt with a cast-steel bed. Top Right: The Scenic Limited, pulled by 4-8-4 No. 1800, needed the assistance of the 3612 to ascend the 3% grade at Mitchell, CO, in 1949. After a crew change and replenishing its tender, the huge articulated will follow the Arkansas River to Pueblo. (HKVC, 3612; LEM, 3612).

49

*Capable of pulling sixteen heavyweight cars up a 1.4% grade at 40 m.p.h., the 1800s had few peers. Originally assigned to the Scenic Limited between Denver and Salt Lake City, they also worked over the Moffat Tunnel route with the Exposition Flyer until diesel-electric units replaced them. The 1800s were the first D&RGW locomotives to have one-piece cast-steel frames, Baldwin driving wheel centers, and roller bearings on all engine and tender axles. The 1800's Royal Gorge consist in 1950 included a heavyweight RPO car, an ex-Chesapeake & Ohio dome-coach and a heavy old diner, all rolling eastward near Florence, CO. (RWA).*

51

In 1946 the 1801 awaits its train in Salt Lake City while the 1802, with the westbound Royal Gorge, was at Salida in 1950. (LEM, HKVC)

The 3700s were delivered at Pueblo in 1938, and were broken in hauling freight trains between there and Denver, before they were sent to their intended territory between Grand Junction and Salt Lake City where they replaced the 1500-series 4-8-2s. On an early trip the 3700 was pulling a northbound freight train up the 1.4% grade north of Colorado Springs. Because these locomotives were equipped with roller bearings on all axels, they could run at passenger train speeds, and they were so powerful that they did not need a helper anywhere, except on the northern flank of Tennessee Pass. One of them, kept polished like the 3705, above, was assigned the Scenic Limited between Dnever and Salt Lake City for a short time, but was withdrawn in fabor of the 1800-series 4-8-4s. (3700 OCP, 3705 HKVC).

The steepest part of the eastern ascent to Soldier Summit was the 2.4% grade near Kyune in Price River canyon, where the 3702 was laboring uphill at only 10 mph, despite the assistance of two compound-expansion 2-8+8-2s—3402 and 3509—shoving at the rear of the 47 car train. 3705 RHK

Aware that the 2-10-2s and compound-expansion 2-8+8-2s were unsuitable for merchandise traffic which was developing prior to World War II, the railroad's trustees bought ten 4-6+6-4s which were the heaviest and most powerful of that type. Having 70-inch drivers, they were much faster than the 4-8-2s used between Grand Junction and Helper, and they were more powerful than the 2-8+8-2s on the steep grades of Soldier Summit. Their initial trips were made between Pueblo and Denver. At this location in 1883, the Denver and Rio Grande/Rio Grande Western narrow-gauge system was completed in the desert of eastern Utah. Six decades later, the 3703 was rolling through Desert Switch enroute to Green River, 13 miles to the east. RHK

These two photos illustrate the effectiveness of the LeChatelier water brake, which was installed on all D&RGW standard-gauge locomotives. The 3619 was easing its long train down the 3% grade near Pando, CO, at 15 mph, without a trace of brake shoe smoke. At Gilluly, UT, on a sub-zero day the 3610 was drifting down the 2% grade at 20 mph. Note the puffs of condensed steam emerging from the cylinder drain cocks, and the faint plume of exhaust-steam coming out of the stack, indicating perfect operation of the water-brake. (3619, RRA, 3610, RTS)

SOLDIER
SUMMIT

Some of the 3600s, displaced by diesel-electric power, were used between Helper and Thistle to help the 3700s up to Soldier Summit, where the 3705 was drifting while the 3601 was still working hard at the rear. The original line with a 4% grade was located at the foot of the hill in the background. RHK

# The War Years
## 1939-1945

4

By the end of 1938 the Rio Grande had completed its acquisitions of new motive power, and it began to modify older engines as they went through the shops for overhaul. Thermic syphons were installed in fireboxes to increase the direct heating area, thus increasing the amount of steam produced, and, hence, the engine's horsepower. The low-pressure cylinders with slide valves were replaced with new ones having piston valves, which increased the engines' power at operating speeds. Engines 3400-3403, 3409 and 3414 received new boilers, which increased their weight to 485,000 lbs., and compound air pumps were installed on all of the 3400s. During 1941, when the first multiple-unit diesel electric locomotives began to arrive, the D&RGW possessed an impressive array of powerful steam engines. The oldest ones were forty immense 4-8-2s, ten of which, having three cylinders, were the heaviest of that wheel arrangement. Five of the nineteen 4-8-4s were the equal of those on much larger railroads. Ten of the most powerful 4-6+6-4s hauled freight

trains in Utah, and sixteen compound-expansion 2-8+8-2s worked as helpers on the steepest grades. Twenty single-expansion 2-8+8-2s, among the most powerful of their type, were assigned to mainline freight service in Colorado. Add to these the smaller and older 4-6-2s, 2-8-2s, and 2-6+6-2s. The railroad appeared to have been very well equipped to handle the growing traffic generated by the war in Europe, but everything changed when the United States entered the war in December 1941. Previously, the preponderant traffic flow was eastward; now, it was westward, causing a major revision of operating techniques. The forward engines of the 3600s, which had experienced frame breakage, were rebuilt

with integrally-cast cylinders and machinery beds. All of these modifications extended over several years, and were completed during 1945.

On the mainline across Utah the 4-cylinder 4-6+6-4s were outperforming the 3-cylinder 4-8-2s. At low speeds, they could haul 50% more tonnage, and at operating speeds they could produce 6000 drawbar-horsepower, twice that of the 4-8-2s. Moreover, the 1600s were aging; so five more articulateds were ordered from Baldwin to replace them. Numbered 3710-3714, they arrived in early 1942, but the 1600s were retained to handle the increased war traffic. The new locomotives were very much like the first ones, the principal difference having been the installation of an exhaust-steam injector in place of the

feedwater heater. This increased the load on the No. 6 driving axle from an already too heavy 74000 lbs. to 75000 lbs. which did not make the track maintenance department any happier. Also, in 1942 two Norfolk & Western 2-6+6-2s were purchased for coal mine runs out of Helper, UT. Erected originally in 1916, these two Mallets were larger than those of the D&RGW, and they were equipped with 12-wheel tenders. Three of the earliest small Mallets were scrapped just after the war, but the others remained active until 1950-1952, when diesel-electric units replaced them.

The three A-B-B-A diesel-electric sets received in 1941 and five more delivered in 1942 were assigned between Denver and Salt Lake City via

*Much lighter merchandise trains were operated with a 2-8+8-2 (No. 3507) ahead of the road engine, usually a 4-6+6-4 (No. 3709). In this scene just west of Castle Gate, UT, the pair of powerful articulateds were making passenger train speed of 30 mph with 44 cars on the steep ascent to Soldier Summit. (RHK).*

*Commencing in 1939 and continuing during the war years, the D&RGW's shops replaced the low-pressure slide-valve cylinders with new ones having piston valves. At the same time syphons were installed in the firebox and combustion changer of the 3400-series 2-8+8-2s, thus improving their efficiency. New boilers were obtained for six of these big articulateds during the war. These older Mallets, like the 3405 and 3508, seen at Alamosa in 1948, were well suited to the 3% grades and many sharp curves on the branch over Wagon Creek Pass between La Veta and Alamosa. Note the different locations for the compound air-pumps. Both of these engines worked for 38 years before they were retired. (HKVC, 3405, 3408).*

the Moffat Tunnel, and the westward flow of traffic required them to haul freight trains up the two worst gradients—the eastern sides of the tunnel and Soldier Summit. The only possible solution to prevent stagnation was to increase train tonnage, and this was accomplished by adding a steam helper to each train, commencing in 1945, when eight compound-expansion 2-8+8-2s were purchased from the Norfolk & Western, which had been replacing its oldest engines with home-built 2-6+6-4s and 2-8+8-2s. Fortunately, these engines built by Baldwin or the N&W's shops, were also almost identical to the D&RGW's 3500-series 2-8+8-2s. They had the same stream pressure, boil-

er diameter, grate area, cylinder size and driver diameter; so, they were given numbers 3550-3557. Although they had 16000-gal. 12-wheel tenders, the Rio Grande added 10000 gal. tank cars to avoid stopping for water at Pinecliffe, 38 miles from Denver on the Denver & Salt Lake railroad.

The Rio Grande wanted also five more 4-6+6-4s, but the War Production Board diverted six Union Pacific 4-6+6-4s from an order being produced by the American Locomotive Company. These locomotives could develop the same horsepower as the 3700s at operating speeds, but they were slightly lighter and could exert less tractive effort at lower speeds. Because

they were accompanied by 25000 gallon/28 ton 4-10 rigid frame tenders, they were confined to the relatively straight track between Grand Junction and Helper. Not wanting to keep these "non-standard" machines, the railroad leased them from a Federal agency and identified them as 3800-3805. In 1946, they were returned to the government, which sold them to the Atlantic Coast Line/Louisville & Nashville railroads, which assigned them to their subsidiary, the Clinchfield railway.

The 4-6+6-4s remained in service between Grand Junction and Salt Lake City until their complete replacement by diesel electric units in 1951. Those which were not scrapped (3700, 3703, 3708, 3710-3713) were transferred to Pueblo where they worked to Denver, Minturn and La Veta, but by the end of 1955 all of them had been set aside for scrapping.

The arrival of additional diesel-electric road-service units enabled the D&RGW to cope with traffic during 1944, but when the war ended in 1945, the Rio Grande went back to the N&W for seven more of the 1918-1924 vintage Mallets. They were numbered 3558-3564, and like the earlier ones, they were utilized as mainline helpers. As traffic subsided to normal levels they were set aside, most of them in 1947. Yet two of them were active until 1950.

The acquisition of more ponderous Mallets did not entirely eliminate the Rio Grande's motive power deficiencies. Troop trains had been pulled by the 1500-series 4-8-2s and often they were double-headed. Regular passenger trains had become so heavy that they required a pair of 4-8-4s to maintain schedules. There was no possibility of obtaining any AT&SF 4-8-4s from Baldwin, UP 4-8-4s from American or SP 4-8-4s from Lima, and the production of 4-8-2s was mostly confined to railroad shops. Coincidentally, it just so happened that the N&W was disposing of its home-made, but unwanted, big 4-8-2s, then 18 years old. The Richmond, Fredericksburg & Potomac, in desperation, bought six of these monsters and the D&RGW took the remaining four. The choice could hardly have been better. Their boilers and feedwater heaters were like those of the 1600s; the cylinders and drivers were the same as those of the 1500s. A slightly larger firebox and greater steam pressure gave them somewhat more tractive effort and drawbar-horsepower. Given numbers 1550-1553, they went to work west of Grand Junction. By 1948, they were no longer needed and were sold to the Wheeling & Lake Erie.

| Year | Road Numbers | Wheel Arrangement | Driver Diameter | Weight of Engine | Tractive Effort | Builder |
|------|------|------|------|------|------|------|
| 1942 | 3350-3351 | 2-6+6-2 | 57 | 427,000 | 76000 | ALC |
|  | 3710-3714 | 4-6+6-4 | 70 | 642,000 | 105000 + 10000 RB | BLW |
| 1943 | 3550-3557 | 2-8+8-2 | 56 | 526,000 | 109000 |  |
|  | 3800-3805 | 4-6+6-4 | 69 | 627,000 | 97000 + 9000 RB | ALC |
| 1945 | 1550-1553 | 4-8-2 | 63 | 402,000 | 69000 | ROA |
|  | 3558-3564 | 2-8+8-2 | 56 | 526,000 | 109000 |  |

Notes:
1550-1553, 3550, 3556, 3558 and 3559 were built at N&W's Roanoke Shops.
3350, 3351 and 3800-3805 were built by American.
3551-3555, 3557, 3560-3564 and 3710-3714 were built by Baldwin
1550-1553 had Worthington feedwater heaters.
3350, 3351 and 3550-3564 were compound -expansion Mallets.
3710-3714 and 3800-3805 were single-expanson articulates.

The two 2-6+6-2s, which were purchased from the Norfolk & Western in 1942, had the same size driving wheels as did the Rio Grande's 2-6+6-2s, but they were heavier and could exert greater tractive effort. They worked in Helper, assembling trains of coal, which had been mined in that productive region.  HKVC

The fifteen 2-8+8-2s, which were obtained from the Norfolk & Western, were very much like the D&RGW's 3500s, having almost identical boilers and fireboxes.  Minor differences in machinery dimensions gave them almost equal tractive efforts; hence, they were numbered 3550-3564.  The first eight engines were used as helpers on the Moffat Tunnel line between Denver and Tabernash; the other seven came two years later, and were sent to Utah for helping westbound freight trains between Helper and Soldier Summit.  The most visible difference was their larger tenders with 6-wheel trucks.  The 3560, with an auxiliary water car, was working out of Denver in 1948.  No. 3562, passing through Pueblo in 1947, appears to have been provided with footboards on the pilot for transfer service among the various yards and local industries.  HKVC

The six 3800s were diverted from a Union Pacific order in 1943 by a Federal agency which leased them to the Rio Grande. Not only were they entirely different mechanically from the 3700s, but they were less powerful. The D&RGW used them for only three years between Grand Junction and Helper, releasing 3700s to work over Soldier Summit into Salt Lake City. The 3802 was still active in March 1946, but by July all of them were stored at Salt Lake City, awaiting movement to some other railroad, which was not the Union Pacific. (HKVC)

The N&W didn't like its 4-8-2s, which were intended for fast freight service, because they damaged the track at operating speeds; so, they were pleased to sell four of them to the D&RGW in 1945. Their boilers were like those of the 1600s, and the firebox and machinery were close to those of the 1500s. Although they performed adequately between Grand Junction and Helper, the 1550-1553 were sold in 1948, when this photo was taken at Salida and Denver. (HKVC)

The 1200-series 2-8-2s were rarely seen on the line over Tennessee Pass, but on this occasion one of the 2-8+8-2s had assisted the 1203 from Pueblo to the summit. From there the track was downhill all of the way to Grand Junction, and the smaller engine's water-brake could control the speed quite well. Descending the 3% grade at Mitchell, the small engine was restraining a 20-car troop train at a comfortable 20 m.p.h. (RHK).

# The End of Standard Gauge Steam 1946-1956

5

The Rio Grande emerged from the war years in remarkably good physical and financial condition, and during 1946 plans were made to terminate the federal trusteeship with a corporate re-organization. Several subsidiary companies were merged into a new corporation in mid-1947, but only one of them—the Denver & Salt Lake contributed any motive power to the "new" D&RGW railroad. A solitary 4-6-0, nine 2-8-0s and ten 2-8-2s were not unusual, but sixteen 2-6+6-0s were unique in the western hemisphere. Not only were these engines larger and heavier than the Rio Grande's 2-6+6-2s, but also their grate-area was 40% greater, giving them more power at operating speeds. These engines were so well adapted to the 2% gradient of the Moffat Tunnel Line, as well as the almost continuous 12° curvature of the convoluted track between Orestod and Toponas, that some of them remained in service until 1952, after 43 years of

continuous service. Though small by 1947 criteria, they were the "super-power" of their era, ranking with the biggest engines in the Rocky Mountains.

The new management began to eliminate steam power gradually and economically, discarding locomotives which needed major repairs or periodic overhaul, while retaining serviceable engines wherever they could be utilized. The process would span a decade, though it had really commenced in 1944, when one of the 3400s was scrapped. Two years later, one of the 3300s vanished and in 1947 the first 3500s and 3550s followed. In 1948 the 1550s were sold and the 3800s were returned to a federal agency for resale. The 1200s, 1220s and 1600s lost members in that year also. The ranks of the 800s, 1500s and 3360s began to thin in 1949 and the 1600s were eliminated completely. In 1950, 1700s and 3350s departed on one-way trips to the scrap-

The 1527 at Leyden. LEM

yards. Two groups became extinct in 1951—the 3500s and 3550s—and the first 3700 was retired. Thus far the powerful 1400s and 1800s had escaped demolition but both groups began to diminish and the last compound—articulateds—3300s, 3350s, 3360s and 3400s—were seen no more on the Rio Grande.

The D&RGW issued its annual steam locomotive summary on January 1, 1953; and it is interesting to note what engines had been kept in useful service. The total came to 124, of which there were 46 old 2-8-0s, whose replacement by diesel-electric units was not yet economically justified. The next largest group was the 20 formidable 3600s, which were unsurpassed as mainline helpers in Colorado. Fourteen 4-8-4s were still working, as were sixteen 4-8-2s and twelve 2-8-2s. These last three groups had been redistributed and could have been found on unfamiliar trackage—branch lines to Craig, Alamosa and Ogden, as well as mainline local freight trains. The eight 1400s were probably stored, but the six 3700s had been sent to Pueblo, Co. for further service. The last of the 800s departed in 1953, followed by the 1800s in 1954;

and in the following year there were no more 1400s or 1500s existing.

The end of all standard-gauge steam power on the railroad became evident in 1955, when the first 3600s were scrapped after almost thirty years of unsurpassed performance. At the beginning of 1956 there were 33 standard-gauge steam locomotives on the roster, 21 of which were 2-8-0s of 1906 and 1908 vintage, used mostly for switching in terminals. A little less aged were 2-8-2s, 1207 (44 years) and 1229 (40 years). The three 2-8+8-2s 3609, 3612, and 3619 were comparatively young— 29 and 26 years of experience, as were the 4-8-4s 1700, 1701 and 1707 at 27 years. Of the four 4-6+6-4s 3700 and 3708 had served for 18 years, while the 3711 and 3712 were "almost-new" at 14 years.

Last of the super-power engines, the three 3600s worked as rear-end helpers from Tabernash to the Moffat Tunnel until the end of October. They ran light to Denver, then were hauled dead to Pueblo. The last steam operation of all was an Alamosa-South Fork turn at the end of December, using the 1151, the last 2-8-0 built for the railroad in 1908. Though these events marked the elimi-

nation of steam power on the Rio Grande's standard gauge lines, the D&RGW was not 100% converted to internal-combustion motive power. It still operated 24 2-8-2s on its narrow-gauge lines between Alamosa and Silverton. But, that's another story.

It is unfortunate that not one of the Rio Grande's superlative steam locomotives has been preserved for us to see and appreciate today. All that remains are photographs and text, which no matter how well composed, is inadequate to "bring them back to life." Those of us who never saw them can find a close resemblance to the 1800s in CB&Q 5629 at the Colorado Railroad Museum in Golden, CO. UP 3985 at Cheyenne, WY can be perceived as a slightly reduced version of the 3700s and N&W 2156 in the National Museum of Transport at Kirkwood, MO is an improved descendent of the 3400s. But there is nothing even close to one of the mighty 3600s, which even remotely resembles those super-power articulateds. All of those marvelous locomotives have vanished, together with those who designed, constructed, operated and maintained them. The efficient diesel-electric units which superseded them never could match the dramatic performance of those super-power steam locomotives!

## Adjusted Tonnage Ratings

| FROM | TO | Class L-131 L-132 Engines 3600-3619 | Class L-107 Engines 3500-3509 | Class L-105 Engines 3700-3709 | Class L-95 Engines 3400-3415 | Class F-81 Engines 1400-1409 | Class M-75 M-67 Engines 1600-1609 | Class M-64 M-67 Engines 1501-1510 1521-1530 1700-1713 | Class K-59 Engines 1200-1213 | Class C-48 Engines 1131-1199 | Class P-44 Engines 800-805 | Class C-38-39-41 Engines 901-925 1000-1029 | Class T-29 Engines 762-793 | Adjustment Factor |
|---|---|---|---|---|---|---|---|---|---|---|---|---|---|---|
| | | Tons | Tons | Tons | Tons | Tons | Tons | Tons | Tons | Tons | Tons | Tons | Tons | Tons |
| Salida | Tennessee Pass | 3000 | 2650 | | 2000 | | 1800 | 1600 | 1210 | 1070 | 1010 | 940 | | 4 |
| Minturn | Tennessee Pass | 1350 | 1100 | | 950 | | 780 | 685 | 550 | 450 | | 420 | | 2 |
| Grand Jct | Glenwood | 5100 | 4850 | 4500 | 3700 | | 3350 | 3000 | 2400 | 2000 | 1750 | 1750 | 1270 | 6 |
| Glenwood | Minturn | 3300 | 2950 | 2650 | 2400 | | 2000 | 1700 | 1500 | 1200 | 1075 | 1130 | 650 | 4 |
| Glenwood | Bond | 3500 | | | 2550 | | | 1825 | 1600 | 1280 | 1150 | | 700 | 6 |
| Grand Jct | Mounds | 4400 | | 3200 | | 2925 | 2525 | 2315 | 1790 | 1630 | | | | 5 |
| Mounds | Helper | 4600 | 3850 | 3700 | 3400 | 3150 | 2750 | 2500 | 1970 | 1630 | | | | 5 |
| Helper | Woodside | 6000 | 5300 | 4600 | 4550 | 4100 | 3670 | 3300 | 2390 | 2100 | | | | 7 |
| Woodside | Green River | 4400 | | 3650 | | 3380 | 3020 | 2700 | 2040 | 1870 | | | | 6 |
| Green River | Grand Jct | 4400 | | 3050 | | 2925 | 2525 | 2315 | 1790 | 1630 | | | | 5 |
| Mounds | Whites | | 2190 | | 1900 | | | | 1010 | 850 | | 700 | | 3 |
| Whites | Sunnyside | | 1325 | | 1030 | | | | 530 | 450 | | 350 | | 2 |
| Grand Jct | Delta | | | | | | | | 4000 | 3320 | | 2720 | 2100 | 10 |
| Delta | Montrose | | | | | | | | 1950 | 1570 | | 1280 | 975 | 5 |
| Delta | Somerset | | | | | | | | | 1520 | | 1240 | 1000 | 5 |
| Somerset | Rogers Mesa | | | | | | | | | 2830 | | 2380 | 1750 | 8 |
| Glenwood | Leon | | | | | | | | | | | | | 4 |
| Leon | Aspen | | | | | | | | | | | | | 3 |

### TONNAGE RATINGS

These ratings are the usual tonnage ratings for dead freight trains. Chief Dispatchers are authorized to increase or decrease these ratings in their discretion in accordance with standing instructions, to adjust for slack grades, condition of power, necessity for maintaining stock schedules, or for any other reasons which justify.

In computing tonnage, the adjustment factor represents the number of tons, which shall be added to the total weight of each car loaded or empty. The caboose shall count as a car. Tonnage hauled may exceed the rating by a fraction of a car.

Following are the car limits per train Tennessee Pass to Minturn:
  Ice trains—55 cars.
  90 loaded cars.
  100 loads and empties mixed.
  100 empties.
  Not to exceed 10 flat cars loaded with steel rails.

1938

| Year | Road Numbers | Wheel Arrangement | Boiler Pressure | Driver Diameter | Weight of Engine | Tractive Effort | Builder |
|---|---|---|---|---|---|---|---|
| 1947 | 1220-1227 | 2-8-2 | 200 | 70 | 295,000 | 63000 | Lima - 1917 |
| 1947 | 1228-1229 | 2-8-2 | 200 | 63 | 306,000 | 63000 | ALC - 1916 |
| 1947 | 3360-3369 | 2-6+6-0 | 225 | 72 | 360,000 | 76000 | ALC - 1909-10 |
| 1947 | 3370-3375 | 2-6+6-0 | 225 | 72 | 360,000 | 76000 | ALC - 1913-16 |

Notes:
1220-1227 were built by Lima in 1915.
1228-1229 were built by American in 1916.
3360-3369 were built by American in 1909-1910 as 0-6+6-0 for the Denver, North Western & Pacific. They were modified by the Denver & Salt Lake in 1913.
3370-3375 were built by American for the D&SL in 1913-1916.
1220-1229 were D&SL 400-409.
3360-3369 were D&SL 200-209; ex-DNW&P 200-209.
3370-3375 were D&SL 211-216.
Ever since 1933, when the Virginian scrapped its twelve 2-6+6-0s, these were the only ones of that wheel-arrangement operated in North America.

December 26, 1956, Bob Richardson went to South Fork, CO to record No. 1151 (the D&RGW's "newest" 2-8-0) turning on the wye before returning to Alamosa, thus bringing an end to standard-gauge steam operations. (RWR)

None of the railroad's magnificent super-power locomotives were preserved, but by a strange circumstance, one 2-8-0 of 1890 vintage was rescued and restored for exhibition at the Colorado Railroad Museum. (RWR)

After 1950, as more diesel-electric units were delivered and more steam locomotives were scrapped, the remaining steam power was relocated or assigned to unusual duties. The most surprising of these was the movement of seven 3700s from Utah to Pueblo, whence they ran to Denver, La Veta and Salida or Minturn. The 1700s hauled local freight trains; 1500s pulled short passenger trains and pushed freight consists; 1200s performed switching chores. Many engines, enroute to the steel mills, worked their way across the system and were seen in strange locations only once before their demise. With but few exceptions, every class of D&RGW locomotive appeared in Alamosa during the final months of the standard-gauge steam era. There was reason for this interesting situation. Locomotives from terminals in Colorado were sent to Pueblo, thence to the Colorado Fuel & Iron Company steel mill at Minnequa. Many of them worked their way on freight trains to Pueblo, and were held there until the scrap yard could accept them. Meanwhile, they were used on freight trains to Alamosa, thus providing the local residents with a continuous display of engines never seen there previously.

Even before the D&RGW had replaced D&SL engines with diesel units, some of the D&SL's locomotives replaced older D&RGW power. The 1227 was relocated to the terminal at Helper, UT, and the 3366 went to its new home at Salt Lake City, replacing one of the Rio Grande's aged 2-6+6-2s. (RWA)

74

The acquisition of the Denver & Salt Lake in 1947 added about 50 miles of 2% grade track, 53 tunnels, 25 miles of line with 12° curvature and 37 locomotives which had been constructed between 1907 and 1916. The ten 2-8-2s, somewhat more powerful than the D&RGW's 1200s, were numbered 1220-1229, and two of them had Coffin feedwater heaters mounted on the front of the smokebox, as seen on No. 1220 at Denver in 1950 after a cosmetic overhaul. This engine was used for another three years before its retirement. The most interesting engines were sixteen compound-expansion 2-6+6-0s, the only ones existing in North America. The first ten (3360-3369) had been built in 1908-1910 as 0-6+6-0s using saturated steam; the others were 2-6+6-0s equipped with superheaters. Note the disc centers on the main driving wheels of the 3374, which lasted only two years as a D&RGW locomotive. Capable of exerting a 76000 lbs. tractive effort and running easily through the almost continuous curvature between Orestod and Toponas, they were irreplaceable until diesel electric units were obtained in 1951. (HKVC, 1220, 3374).

The 3361 was 40 years old when this photo of it was taken as it descended the 2% grade south of Plainview, CO. It had been rebuilt in 1913 with a leading truck and superheater. (RWA)

In 1956, the last year of standard-gauge steam operations, the 3609 was the D&RGW's oldest articulated, with a 29-year career. At Winter Park, CO, it was hauling am eastbound freight train up to Moffat Tunnel, with an unusually clear stack  (LEM)

On October 26, 1956, Otto Perry was at Tollad, CO, watching the D&RGW's last two articulateds—3619 and 3609—make their final trip from Tabernash to Denver, this marked the end of a 43-year super power era on the D&RGW. (OCP)

In late 1946 the 3613 was still the primary freight hauler between Grand Junction and Denver, though it required two helpers to surmount the northern side of Tennessee Pass. (RHK)

The 3700s were unknown in Salida until 1951 when seven of them were transferred from Utah to Pueblo and operated to Denver, Salida and La Veta. Sometimes they would take a freight train over Tennessee Pass as far as Minturn, but there are no known photos of them north of Salida. (3701 HKVC, 3708 NRM)

The presence of 1403 in Alamosa is difficult to explain because this Utah line's 2-10-2 had such a long rigid wheelbase, unsuitable for the sharp curvature of the track over Wagon Creek. It is possible that the huge engine was in Pueblo awaiting scrapping, when someone wondered if it could actually negotiate the sharply curved track between La Veta and Alamosa. (RWR)

The 1202 owed its longevity to the sale of the 2-8-0 which had been the yard switcher at Montrose, the end of the branch from Grand Junction. Because two narrow-gauge lines terminated there the trackage was 3-rail, which necessitated the use of an idler car having two couplers for cars of either gauge. (RWR)

The 3606 , drifting downgrade with a train of empty gondolas, was passing the 3553 (RHK)

Pushing behind the caboose of the train on the previous page was the 1607, a 3-cylinder 4-8-2 from Utah; three years later, it would become the sole survivor of its class. (RHK)

Demoted from mainline helper duties to transfer switching at Pueblo, the 3562 was the last of the 2-8+8-2s obtained from the N&W to remain active. In the background 4-8-4 No. 1800 awaiting departure with the westbound Royal Gorge. (RWA)

In their final years of service, the ex-Norfolk and Western compound-expansion 2-8+8-2s worked as mid-train or rear end helpers on the 3% grade between Minturn and Tennessee Pass. (LEM)

The 3375 was the last active 2-6+6-0 was descended the 2% grade at Rocky, with a noticable lack of smoke. (LEM)

# D&RGW 3703
## Born March 1938-Died October 1952

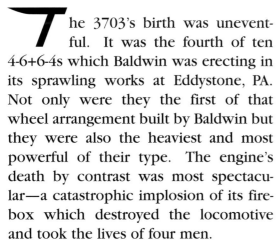

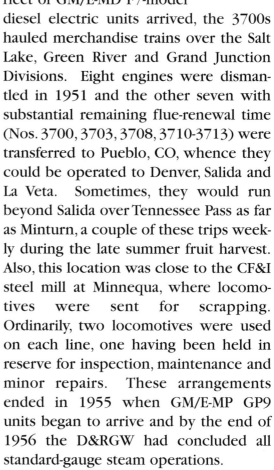

The 3703's birth was uneventful. It was the fourth of ten 4-6+6-4s which Baldwin was erecting in its sprawling works at Eddystone, PA. Not only were they the first of that wheel arrangement built by Baldwin but they were also the heaviest and most powerful of their type. The engine's death by contrast was most spectacular—a catastrophic implosion of its firebox which destroyed the locomotive and took the lives of four men.

They were enormous locomotives and only marginally surpassed in weight and size by the Northern Pacific's Class Z8 engines. They had the same grate area as the D&RGW's huge L131/132 single-expansion 2-8+8-2s (137 sq. ft.) and a boiler almost as large (102 vs. 108 inches in diameter). Engine lengths differed by only 14 inches and total weights by just 23,000 pounds (73'4"/74'6", 642,000/665,000 lbs.). Having been equipped with roller bearings on all axles, the L105 could exert a zero-speed tractive effort of 115,000 lbs. and produce 6000 drawbar horsepower at 30-35 mph. In passenger service they were allowed to run at 80 mph and 60 mph with freight trains.

Together with five other slightly different 4-6+6-4s delivered from Baldwin in 1942 (Nos. 3710-3714) these locomotives generated 2/3 of the ten-miles over the Wasatch Mountains between Salt Lake City and Helper, UT, (215 miles) and across the desert to Grand Junction, CO. (177 miles). Replacing various combinations of 2-8-2s and heavy 4-8-2s, they increased train speeds and reduced coal and water consumption, as well as helper mileage on both flanks of Soldiers Summit.

Until 1949 when the fleet of GM/E-MD F7-model diesel electric units arrived, the 3700s hauled merchandise trains over the Salt Lake, Green River and Grand Junction Divisions. Eight engines were dismantled in 1951 and the other seven with substantial remaining flue-renewal time (Nos. 3700, 3703, 3708, 3710-3713) were transferred to Pueblo, CO, whence they could be operated to Denver, Salida and La Veta. Sometimes, they would run beyond Salida over Tennessee Pass as far as Minturn, a couple of these trips weekly during the late summer fruit harvest. Also, this location was close to the CF&I steel mill at Minnequa, where locomotives were sent for scrapping. Ordinarily, two locomotives were used on each line, one having been held in reserve for inspection, maintenance and minor repairs. These arrangements ended in 1955 when GM/E-MP GP9 units began to arrive and by the end of 1956 the D&RGW had concluded all standard-gauge steam operations.

In the fall of 1952 engines 3700 and 3703 had been handling fast freight trains No. 67 (southward) and No. 68 (northward) between Pueblo and Denver. Other than some minor problems with the 3703's feedwater pump lubrication during August, the locomotive performed satisfactorily. On October 17th, it had pulled a full-tonnage train to Denver, and the engine crew reported that the boiler had steamed well, that the feedwater pump had no difficulty in maintaining the water level between 1/2 and 3/4 in the sight-glass and that there were no leaking staybolts or boiler tubes.

The 3609 is eastbound at Winter Park in 1956 (LEM)

The engineer had tested the injector at Pueblo and found that it was functioning properly. Other than a temporarily stuck throttle at Palmer Lake, the trip was uneventful and the locomotive appeared to have been in perfect operational condition. The defective throttle was repaired at Burnham Shops (Denver) on the 18th and the engine was assigned to No. 67 on the morning of the 19th.

In the small hours of the 19th the Burnham Yard crew assembled Train 67—31 loaded cars, 64 empties and caboose—3850 actual/4240 adjusted tens. The train weight was well beyond the 3703's 2650-ten rating; so a two-unit B-B GM/E-MD FT/F3 helper was scheduled to follow the train as far as Sedalia, then couple behind the caboose while the 3703 stopped to replenish its water supply. The diesel electrics would push the train up the 1.4% grade to the summit at Palmer Lake, turn on the wye, and return light to Burnham. Meanwhile, the round house hostlers had built a fire in the 3703's firebox, filled its boiler with 7200 gallons of hot water, and loaded the tender with 26 tons of coal and 20,000 gallons of water. At about 10:00 a.m. No. 67 was ready for air-brake inspection and the customary checking of train and engine by the train and locomotive

crews. The engineer checked the injector, and the fireman operated the feedwater pump and stoker controls. The water-level sight-glasses were half full, and at 10:25 A.M. the conductor gave the highball signal for departure.

The 50-mile profile of the D&RGW/AT&SF southbound track was almost entirely uphill from Burnham Yard (5241 ft. elevation) to the summit at Palmer Lake (7237 ft.). At Englewood, 5 miles south of the yards, the gradient increased from less than 1/2% to 1%, and at Sedalia, 17 miles farther, the maximum gradient became an almost unbroken 1.42% to Palmer Lake. Over the entire ascent the 3703 would be required to produce somewhat more than 6000 drawbar-horsepower to maintain a 30-mph train speed, the equivalent of a Union Pacific 4-8+8-4 at 25 mph. Its boiler would convert 12,500 gallons of water into 255-PSI steam hourly, a quantity which would be easily supplied by either the engineer's injector or the fireman's positive-displacement feedwater pump. The few downgrade stretches of track were so short that they provided no relief for the 3703's exertions, but one of them would determine its ultimate fate.

After responding to the conductor's signal, the engineer moved all four Walschaerts valve-gears to the maximum tractive effort position, released the locomotive and train brakes, and began to open the front-end throttle. Ever so slowly, the 3703 stretched the train with its 115,000-pound drawbar pull and Train 67 was on its way toward Pueblo. The fireman adjusted the stoker feed, opened the feedwater pump's steam-supply valve one turn. He noted the pump delivery pressure and glanced at the water level and steam pressure gauges. Thus commenced what appeared to have been a routine run. Now, this was a Sunday and the engine crew were watching for photographers at the several grade crossings as far as Littleton, as well as for cars which were pacing the train on the highway adjacent to the tracks on the engineer's side. After crossing the AT&SF track at South Denver Junction—2 miles from Burnham—the engineer opened the throttle fully and changed the valve gears' travel to accelerate the train to its normal running speed of about 35 mph for the first ten miles of the trip where the gradient was less than 1/2%. Thereafter, the speed would decrease gradually to about 15 mph prior to the stop for water at Sedalia.

Because the engine was not equipped with a low-water alarm the crew was unaware that the feedwater pump had not been turned on fully (four turns of the valve) after the running brake-test at South Denver Junction, and consequently the cylinders were drawing water from the boiler, lowering its level about an inch every two minutes. At Englewood, no water was showing in the water glasses and at Littleton the level was even with the crown sheet (top of the firebox). If at that point the engineer and fireman had looked at the water glasses, they may have thought that they were full as no attempt was made to operate the injector or to dump the fire. (Empty and full appear the same in tubular water glasses).

After the train had passed over Highway 85 at Wolhurst the train crew must have sensed that there was something amiss. The speed was decreasing too rapidly on the steeper gradient as though the engine was not steaming well. And, indeed it wasn't. At Wolhurst the water level was about 4 inches below the top of the crown sheet, and very little steam was being produced in that uncovered area. Marked by a blue band of overheated steel, the water level would sink another 5 inches, far below the abilities of the combustion chamber syphon and two more in the firebox to circulate enough water from the bottom of the boiler to protect this extremely overheated area. The most critical zone was the triangle formed by the back of the front syphon and the fronts of the rear syphons, where the D&RGW's research people had measured temperatures exceeding 1400 degrees F. So long as the boiler was inclined up-grade the forward syphon could spew a trickle of water over that area where it flashed into super-heated steam. But that uneasy equilibrium ended when the 3703 tilted downward a short segment of almost-1% grade just north of Acequia (MP 17). The time was 11:10 A.M.

During that short descent which consumed about two minutes, that crucial triangle had become so red-hot that no amount of water could have cooled it enough when the engine resumed its upward inclination. Only dumping the fire would have prevented the impending disaster, and probably it was already too late for that to have been effective. By now, the inner ends of the staybolts had lost most of their mechanical strength and were unable to restrain the crown sheet against the force of the steam—255 pounds on each square inch of surface. Gradually the edges of the staybolt holes began to shear off the heads of the staybolts to reform them into cup-shaped end depressions. Thus relieved of its support, the critical area began to bulge downward, forming a crossways elliptical blister. Like a balloon, this blister expanded until the crown sheet was only

No. 3615 is working south-bound at Larkspur in 1954 (LEM)

Pulling out of Burnham with a southbound mixed freight, the 3605 is showing signs of being recently shopped in this 1952 scene. (LEM)

3/32-inch thick, a quarter of the sheet's original thickness. Unable to restrain a force of about 1-million pounds, the blister split open in a downward tear about twelve feet long, bending the adjacent surfaces and opening a gaping hole. Instantaneously, all of the water remaining in the boiler expanded into 1400 times as much steam, and all of it tried to escape at the speed of sound through the opening. A total of some 600 staybolts were decapitated in this initial phase of the implosion, and the sides of the firebox were bulged outward about four inches at the mud-ring on each side.

The force of the downward blast of steam was something in the neighborhood of 1 ½-million pounds and it lasted about a tenth of a second! Grates, arch brick and ash-pan parts were flung as much as 450 feet from the track. The rear frame extension and the flexible connection between the two machinery beds were broken and the rails were indented beneath the rearmost driving wheels and all four trailing-truck wheels. Forty seven 1-1½ inch bolts were broken when the boiler and firebox lifted off the propulsion machinery and began an arched end-over-end flight. The 3703's boiler ended its catastrophic somersault by plunging into the ground beside the track, cab first and upside down about 250 feet ahead of the point where it had become separated. The tender and train came to a stop some 200 feet beyond the boiler; but the forward engine traveled nearly 1/3 mile before stopping. Broken into four fractured segments, the 3703 was beyond resurrection and it would never run again.

Conductor Lundberg was contemplating an uneventful trip when the train's brakes went into emergency. He checked his Hamilton 992B watch—11:10 A.M.—glanced at trackside landmarks to determine his location and looked forward over the train. He saw "a cloud of dust flying" but did not know its origin. He walked forward along the train, noting that a coupler knuckle had broken on the 37th car ahead of the caboose, which would have accounted for the emergency brake application. But having heard no whistle from the engineer to protect the rear of the train, he continued until he saw the 3703's inverted boiler lying beside the track. Staying only long enough to realize that no one had survived the catastrophe, he hurried toward a trackside telephone to report the incident. At 12:32 P.M., Superintendent Coleman sent a teletype message to all those who would be involved subsequently. The Burnham

*804 is leading the westbound Craig local in 1954. (LEMC)*

wrecking train was called to depart at 12:45 and Trainmaster Daly with Assistant Division Engineer Waring went immediately to the site. The county coroner and the railroad's photographer went there also.

Meanwhile, the two following helper units pushed the rear part of the train against the forward segment and the broken knuckle was replaced, thus allowing them to pull the train back to a siding at Acequia. The first car behind the tender was left at the scene to keep the brakeless tender and the two engine chassis from rolling back downhill. The derrick picked up the two chassis and took them with the tender and the car of iron ore back to Burnham Shops but the boiler was left behind because it was too heavy for one derrick. By 7:00 P.M., the track was back in service and Train 67 resumed its run to Pueblo behind diesel-electric units.

As soon as the wrecking crane could be brought from Pueblo to assist Burnham's derrick the boiler was lifted onto two flat-cars and taken to the Burnham Shops, where it was positioned inside for examination by D&RGW and ICC personnel. The locomotive's trucks, both chassis and tender, were placed on a track outside. All of the feedwater equipment—pump, injector, heater—and as much of the piping and valves as had been found were laid out for inspection. All of the piping was found to be open and the valves worked properly. It was at this point that the injector's control valve was found to be closed and that for the feedwater pump was open only one-quarter of maximum. The pump and injector were then installed on the 3700 and were tested in the shops as well as on runs to Pueblo. Both

were able to deliver enough water for maximum-power operation (15000 gallons hourly for the pump and 12500 for the injector).

While these tests were being made the railroad's Research Laboratory was making metallurgical and physical tests on stay-bolts and specimens removed from the crown-sheet adjacent to the fracture. It was found that the steel was of specified thickness, metallic composition and physical properties and there were no mechanical defects. The rupture was ductile, stretched at excessively high temperatures and not brittle like window glass. The same was true for the staybolts. Although the firebox had some welded patches in its sides and ends, none of them were in the path of the crack. Even the grain structure

The 3615 is charging uphill, close to the summit, at Plamer Lake.! (LEM)

of the steel was examined by photo-microscopy, confirming the visual evidence of ductile elongation at elevated temperatures far above normal.

Because they were located at the top of the boiler's backhead, the two water columns and water-level sight-glasses were severely damaged when the boiler struck the ground, leaving a trench about 35 feet long and 3-6 feet deep. These parts which were recovered were found to be clean, unobstructed and open.

The D&RGW's internal report, consisting of four looseleaf volumes, was issued on 20 November. It contained a description of the locomotive and train, the internal correspondence at the time of the accident, texts pertaining to the many exami-nations and tests and descriptions of water-supply equipment. It was illustrated with numerous drawings, diagrams and color-photos. The ICC's report was dated 2 December, and was an almost verbatim copy of the D&RGW's text but lacked any illustrative material. Neither report called attention to the finding that the injector was turned off and that the reciprocating pump had not been turned on to operate at full capacity. The railroad's conclusion was "This explosion was caused by failure of the crown sheet due to a failure to keep water at a level above the crown sheet of the boiler. There were no other contribut-ing causes." The ICC's report differed some-what. "It is found that this accident was caused by an overheated crown sheet due

In another 1954 scene, the 3615 leads a southbound freight at Castle Rock.. (LEM)

The 1527 is shoving hard on the caboose of a westbound train at Leyden, CO in this dramatic view from 1952. (LEM)

3708 Southbound at Salida , CO 1953 (EFG)

to low water." Period.

After the investigations had been completed, the 3703's boiler was stored inverted south of the Burnham roundhouse, and its machinery was parked on a storage track. There these remnants of the locomotive remained until all legal matters concerning the accident had been settled and it was not until June 1955 that the 3703 was formally scrapped. However, it did not vanish entirely; both builder's plates and the front number-plate have been preserved in private collections.

## —R.I.P.—

Among the items in the D&RGW's report were these:

Coupler knuckle replacement - $15
Salvage value of engine and tender -
$11,309.17
Book value of engine -
$188,534.77
Total estimated expense of accident -
$178,834.25

## AUTHOR'S COMMENTARY:

Neither the ICC nor D&RGW reports provided answers for two obvious questions regarding the accident. (1) At South Denver Junction, when the engineer opened the throttle fully, the fireman increased the coal feed-rate of the mechanical stoker accordingly. However, feedwater supply from the pump was not changed from its original setting to maximum capacity. That was the basic cause of the disaster. (2) During the thirty minute period prior to the implosion, the water glasses were empty; yet this dangerous indication went unnoticed, because the engineer did not operate his injector, and the firemen did not dump the fire to prevent the catastrophe.

3703's boiler inverted after it's explosion in October, 1952. (RRA)

RIO GRANDE
ROYAL GORGE
MOFFAT TUNNEL
SCENIC LINE
OF THE
WORLD

3614 Southbound at Red Cliff, 1949
(LEM)

Leading the westbound Royal Gorge
the 1804 is departing Buena Vista,
CO on a bright day in 1950 (LEM)

In 1949, the 3612 was leading and 3400 was working out of Minturn as a rear-end helper on the grade to Tennessee Pass at Mitchell, CO.   LEM

# *Bibliography*

*Rio Grande Steam Locomotives*-Donald Heimburger- Heimburger House 1981. Catalog of standard gauge locomotives, illustrated with builders' and action photos. Includes D&RGW roster diagrams with weight and dimension data. No text.

*Locomotives of the Rio Grande*-Colorado Railroad Museum 1980 illustrated roster of all D&RG-RGW-D&&RGW steam and diesel, narrow and standard gauge. Individual engines are grouped by railroad class with basic group data. Includes all subsidiaries and acquisitions since 1870. Illustrated with 3/4-angle photos.

*Rio Grande...to the Pacific!*-Robert A. LeMassena, Sundance Publications, 1974 contains a chronology of locomotive acquisitions from 1870. Brief note for each year. Includes all subsidiaries and acquisitions, steam and diesel, narrow and standard gauge.

3710 is trying to get it's southbound train in motion departing Burnham in this 1952 scene. (LEM)

3613 and 1503 a working hard through the S curve at Mitchell, CO in a 1949 view. (LEM)